READ-ALOUD
ANTHOLOGY

GRADE 3

ISBN 10 0-15-351785-9

ISBN 13 978-0-15-351785-3

4500235964

READ-ALOUD
ANTHOLOGY

CONTENTS

First Day JITTERS

by Julie Danneberg

"**S**arah, dear, time to get out of bed," Mr. Hartwell said, poking his head through the bedroom doorway. "You don't want to miss the first day at your new school, do you?"

"I'm not going," said Sarah, and pulled the covers over her head.

"Of course you're going, honey," said Mr. Hartwell, as he walked over to the window and snapped up the shade.

"No, I'm not. I don't want to start over again. I don't like my new school," Sarah said. She tunneled down to the end of her bed.

"How can you dislike your new school, sweetheart?" Mr. Hartwell chuckled. "You've never been there before! Don't worry. You liked your other school, you'll like this one. Besides, just think of all the new friends you'll meet."

"That's just it. I don't know anybody, and it will be hard, and . . . I just don't like it, that's all."

"What will everyone think if you aren't there? We told them you were coming!"

"They will think that I am lucky and they will wish that they were at home in bed like me."

Mr. Hartwell sighed. "Sarah Jane Hartwell, I'm not playing this silly game one second longer. I'll see you downstairs in five minutes."

Sarah tumbled out of bed. She stumbled into the bathroom. She fumbled into her clothes.

"My head hurts," she moaned as she trudged into the kitchen.

Mr. Hartwell handed Sarah a piece of toast and her lunchbox. They walked to the car. Sarah's hands were cold and clammy.

VOCABULARY

If one's hands are *clammy*, they are cold, wet, and sticky.

They drove down the street.

She couldn't breathe.

And then they were there.

"I feel sick," said Sarah weakly.

"Nonsense," said Mr. Hartwell. "You'll love your new school once you get started. Oh, look. There's your principal, Mrs. Burton."

Sarah slumped down in her seat.

"Oh, Sarah," Mrs. Burton gushed, peeking into the car. "There you are. Come on. I'll show you where to go."

She led Sarah into the building and walked quickly through the crowded hallways. "Don't worry. Everyone is nervous the first day," she said over her shoulder as Sarah rushed to keep up.

When they got to the classroom, most of the children were already in their seats.

The class looked up as Mrs. Burton cleared her throat.

"Class. Class. Attention, please," said Mrs. Burton. When the class was quiet she led Sarah to the front of the room and said, "Class, I would like you to meet . . .

. . . your new teacher, Mrs. Sarah Jane Hartwell."

Tiger, Tiger!

by Mona Lee

Oh, no! Tiger, tiger! What are you doing?
Books are for reading, not for chewing.

Stop, tiger, tiger! Don't eat the pages.
This kind of behavior is simply outrageous!

Books are not food for the belly, you see.
They're food for the mind, for you and for me.

Authors write stories and books to be read,
Not gobbled by you as if they were bread!

Tiger, tiger! Please listen and hear what I say!
You mustn't treat books in this terrible way.

The licking and tearing and chomping you do
Is turning fine literature into a stew!

VOCABULARY
To *refrain* is to hold back from doing an activity.

Eating paper will give you an ache and a pain—
Please, tiger, tiger, I beg you—refrain.

Books are a feast of a different kind,
With so many favorites for us to find.

Charlotte, that spider of E. B. White's
Has a message for us—let's read what she writes.

Beverly Cleary is such a good writer,
With Ramona, Leigh Botts and his loyal dog, Strider.

Eric Carle writes a story and adds pictures to it.
His so-hungry caterpillar eats holes right through it!

Aha, tiger, tiger! It's clear to me now
How to conquer your problem—you'll soon see how.

I'll rest this book gently upon your huge paws
Please hide those big teeth, and retract those sharp claws.

VOCABULARY
To *retract* is to pull back in.

Forget chewing pages—don't take one more bite.
Let *me* turn the pages; use only your sight.

Read over my shoulder; I'll show you the way.
Be ready for tales of the past and today.

We'll read every page, taking in every letter.
Relax by my side. Does your belly feel better?

Click, Clack, Moo is so funny! Let's read it right now.
You'll laugh to see typewriting done by a cow!

VOCABULARY
To *subside* is to become less.

I can see, tiger, tiger, your hunger subside.
Your resistance to eating books fills me with pride.

Is fiction or nonfiction your "cup of tea"?
Give me your paw now, and come with me.

I will take you to places unknown, far away—
Places where imagination can play.

You ask me about this big basket I carry?
I'm taking books back to our local library.

The poems are uneaten; the plays are quite dry.
You've learned to behave and give reading a try.

Would you like to come with me and choose your own book?
There are plenty of stories wherever you look.

Your happy smile shows me that you understand.
Your soft, furry paw is holding my hand.

Good job, tiger, tiger! My work here is done.
Your reading adventure has truly begun!

A One-Room School

by Bobbie Kalman

The Schoolhouse

It may be difficult to believe, but there was a time when few communities had schools. Children were taught at home, at a neighbor's house, or received no education at all. When a community grew and there were a number of children in an area, the settlers gathered together and built a schoolhouse. With hard work and cooperation, a log schoolhouse could be built quickly.

The First Schools

Early schoolhouses had four walls and a roof. One or two windows allowed in just enough sunlight for students to see their work. Long, slanting shelves were attached to the two side walls. These shelves served as desks. Children sat on three-legged stools or simple benches. The teacher's desk, made of rough planks, faced the students. The fireplace barely kept the classroom warm in the winter.

Later Schools

As more families sent their children to school, a larger building was needed. The new school had two entrances—one for the girls and one for the boys. Proper desks were purchased to replace the shelves and benches. The girls sat on one side of the room, and the boys on the other. The youngest children sat at the front of the classroom, close to

VOCABULARY
Proper means
suitable or right.

the teacher. Behind the teacher was a blackboard. A wood stove heated the classroom.

The Teacher Rules!

To become a teacher, a man or woman had to be able to read, write, and handle rough-and-ready students. Most teachers were men. They were called schoolmasters. Female teachers had to be single. Once a woman married, she was not allowed to continue teaching in the school.

Hiring the Teacher

When a new teacher arrived in town, he or she was given food and shelter. Every family in the community paid a small amount of money for the teacher's salary and took turns boarding the teacher. The families that could not pay with money gave the teacher goods such as corn. The goods were then traded for money or other items at the general store.

> **VOCABULARY**
> To *board* is to provide a place to live and to sleep.

Teaching the Children

One teacher instructed all the children in the school. He or she taught as many as eight grades at a time. The class was divided into four groups, each with an upper and lower grade. If there were many children in a community, only the older students were allowed to attend school during the school year. A female teacher was hired to teach the younger children during the summer months.

Keeping Order in the Classroom

The teacher did more than teach the children. He or she also had to keep order in the school. With children of all ages learning different things at the same time, good behavior was important. It was the responsibility of the teacher to punish children who misbehaved.

Reaching for the Moon

by Buzz Aldrin

When Edwin "Buzz" Aldrin was a boy, he learned to persevere. After years of hard work and focusing on his goals, he became one of the first people to walk on the moon. The following is an excerpt from his autobiography, *Reaching for the Moon*.

My first spaceflight was on board *Gemini 12*. Once the spacecraft was in orbit, I put on my space suit, opened the hatch, and drifted out into space. Only a thin cord connected me to *Gemini* as we circled the Earth at 17,500 miles per hour, five miles every second. It took us less than two hours to go all the way around the world.

But the speed didn't seem real to me. I felt as if I were gently floating while the Earth spun beneath me. I could see the great curve of my home planet: the brown mass of Africa, night falling over the Indian Ocean, a shower of green meteors tumbling into the Australian desert.

After *Gemini 12*, there was a new mission—Apollo. The goal of Apollo was to put humans on the Moon.

Many people thought it couldn't be done. They thought that the powerful rockets needed to go that far could never be built. They thought that computers could never do all the calculations. They thought that, even if we did reach the Moon, we would never be able to take off again to come home. But, one by one, all the challenges were met.

Neil Armstrong, Mike Collins, and I were next in line for a spaceflight, so we were chosen as the team for *Apollo 11*—the flight that would land on the moon.

Three years after my Gemini mission, I stood beside *Apollo 11*'s Saturn V rocket. It was sunrise on July 16, 1969. Neil and Mike were already in their places on board. For a few moments I was alone.

All my life I had struggled to learn, to compete, to succeed, so that I could be what I was in that one moment: an astronaut on a mission to the Moon. I felt nothing but calm confidence. I was sure we would make it there and back.

It was time for me to board.

Neil, Mike, and I lay side by side on three couches, tightly strapped in. Beneath us I heard a rumble, like a faraway train. But as we lifted off, the movement felt so gentle that if I had not been looking at the instruments, I would never have known we were on our way.

Outside the window of the *Apollo 11*, the Earth grew smaller and smaller. At last we were so far away that I could hold up my thumb and block the bright disk from my sight.

After five hours we could take off our space suits and helmets and move around the cabin. We ate chicken salad and applesauce for dinner, with shrimp cocktail, my favorite of our freeze-dried choices. Then it was time to rest. Wrapped in sleeping bags, we floated above the couches, comfortably weightless. For this time *Apollo 11* was our home, a tiny bubble of air and warmth speeding through the icy cold of space.

Four days after launch, and after traveling 240,000 miles, we were in orbit around the Moon. *Apollo* separated into two parts: *Columbia*, where Mike would wait in orbit, and the *Eagle*, the lander. The *Eagle* was powerful enough to take Neil and me down to the Moon's surface and back up to *Columbia*. But its walls were so thin, I could have punched a pencil through them if I had tried.

The computer had chosen a spot for the *Eagle* to land. But through the window we could see that it was too rocky. We couldn't rely on the computer to land the *Eagle* safely. We would have to do it ourselves.

Neil took control. I called out to let him know how far we were from the ground. Two hundred feet. One hundred. Forty. By the time the *Eagle* landed, we had used up almost all our fuel with only twenty seconds left to spare.

But we had made it. We were safely on the surface of the Moon. I grinned at Neil. There was no need to say anything. We had work to do.

Flight and spaceflight had always meant motion to me. But now the *Eagle* stood perfectly still.

Neil and I put on our space suits. Neil climbed out first and descended *Eagle*'s ladder to the Moon's surface. Everyone listening back on Earth heard Neil's first words: "That's one small step for . . . man, one giant leap for mankind."

I climbed down the ladder and joined Neil. There was no color on the Moon. A flat landscape of rocks and craters stretched in all directions. Everything was gray or white. The shadows and the sky above were as black as the blackest velvet I had ever seen. I exclaimed: "Magnificent desolation."

VOCABULARY
Desolation is emptiness or loneliness.

I could see Earth, our home, in the sky overhead—blue water, white clouds, and brown land. I could see the continents, and I knew that they were younger than the Moon dust in which Neil and I were now leaving our footprints.

I took out the American flag from the compartment where it was stored.

Neil and I could force the pole only a few inches into the Moon's soil. I knew that more than half a billion people back on Earth were watching on television, and I worried that the flag would sag or tip. But when we took our hands away, it stood straight. I snapped off a crisp salute, just as I was taught at West Point.

SUPPORT UNDERSTANDING
After high school, Buzz Aldrin entered the United States Military Academy at *West Point* to join the Air Force.

We moved quickly on to other tasks. I became a rock collector, gathering samples for study back on Earth. Still, I remember that brief moment perfectly, so many years later. I remember the pride I felt and how I imagined the pride of every American on Earth.

Neil and I set up a plaque that would remain on the surface of the Moon with the simple words:

HERE MEN FROM THE PLANET EARTH

FIRST SET FOOT UPON THE MOON

JULY 1969, A.D.

WE CAME IN PEACE FOR ALL MANKIND

GREAT INVENTIONS: THE TELEVISION

by Marc Tyler Nobleman

Before Television

For thousands of years, people shared messages in simple ways. At first, people traveled between towns to share news. Later, people wrote and sent letters to each other. People carried the letters across the country by foot or on horseback.

Rise of Technology

By the late 1800s, the world was changing. People used more machines. The radio and the telephone were invented. These inventions let people send messages over long distances. By the 1920s, people could enjoy music and shows on the radio.

In the late 1800s, movies were also invented. The moving pictures amazed people. Movies quickly became popular. Scientists looked for ways to send moving pictures over long distances.

Mechanical Television

The mechanical television was an early idea for sending moving pictures over long distances. John Logie Baird from Scotland built a mechanical television in the 1920s. It used a spinning disk that could copy a picture line by line. Then each line could be sent to another disk. That disk would put the image back together.

Inventors of Television

Modern television was invented over many years. Philo T. Farnsworth and Vladimir Zworykin were two early inventors. Their work led to the televisions people watch today.

Television Becomes Popular

Farnsworth and Zworykin's inventions quickly became popular. By the late 1930s, people could buy the first black-and-white televisions. At the same time, the first TV stations formed.

Early Years

Many people saw TVs for the first time at the 1939 New York World's Fair. The first TVs sold for $200 to $600.

New Features

By the 1950s, TVs had many new features. Color TVs went on sale in 1953. The first remote controls were added in the early 1950s. They were attached to the TV by a cable. The first wireless remote control came out in 1956.

Changing Styles

TV styles have changed over the years. Early TVs had small screens. Their parts were tucked in large wooden frames. By the 1970s and 1980s, TVs were built with more plastic. They were made in many shapes and sizes. Today, some TVs can be held in one hand. Others have wide screens like movie screens.

Television Today

The main parts of a television changed very little for 65 years. In recent years, companies have found new ways to create images on TV screens.

Building a Better Picture

Today, digital television is changing the shape and style of TVs. Digital television uses a digital signal to make pictures. Digital signals carry very clear sound and pictures. They also carry pictures that are wider than most TVs can show.

Staying Connected

Many people did not own a TV 65 years ago. Since then, TV has changed our lives. It entertains us. It delivers news. It lets people learn about each other. TV connects people around the world.

Pop's Bridge

by Eve Bunting

My pop is building the Golden Gate Bridge.

Almost every day after school, Charlie Shu and I go to Fort Point and watch. The bridge will stretch across the bay, from San Francisco to Marin. People said this bridge couldn't be built. Some call it the impossible bridge. They say the bay is too deep, the currents too strong, the winds blowing in from the ocean too fierce.

But I know my pop can do it. Whenever I say he's building the bridge, Mom laughs. "There's a crew of more than a thousand men working on that bridge, Robert. Including Charlie's dad," she reminds me. I know that, but I just shrug.

To me, it's Pop's bridge.

Pop's a high-iron man, balancing on the slatted catwalks, spinning and bending the cables. He climbs so high that sometimes clouds come down around his shoulders. When the fog rolls in, he disappears completely. That's why the high-iron men are called skywalkers.

Charlie's dad is a painter. The painters start work long before the bridge is even finished. My pop says if it weren't for them, the bridge would rust away, but I think he's just saying that to be nice. The skywalkers have the most important job of all.

At Fort Point I look for Pop through the binoculars Mom lends me. The workers look alike in their overalls and swabbie hats, but I can always find my pop because of the red kerchief he ties at his throat. It's our own scarlet signal.

I don't worry much about him on days when the sun sparkles on the water, when sailboats skim below. It's so beautiful I can forget that it's dangerous, too. But when the wind blows through the Golden Gate, the men cling to the girders like caterpillars on a branch. On foggy days my hands sweat on the binoculars. *Where is he?* When I find him, I try not to look away, as though the force of my eyes can keep him from falling.

At my house Charlie and I work on a jigsaw puzzle Mom bought us. When it's done it will show how an artist thinks the bridge will look. Charlie and I work on the puzzle most every day. Bending over it I feel like I'm building the real thing, along with Pop. I'm a skywalker, too.

"We're almost done," Charlie says. "I wonder which of us will put in the last piece?"

I shrug. But what he says makes me think. My pop built that bridge. He should set the last puzzle piece in place. That's only fair, even though Charlie might think his dad should do it. When Charlie isn't looking, I slip one of the pieces into my pocket. Later I hide it in my room. I'm saving it for Pop.

The "impossible bridge" is nearly finished. One evening Mom and Pop and I walk down to Fort Point. The bridge hangs between stars and sea.

"It's like a giant harp," my pop says. "A harp for the angels to play." I look up at him, and I can tell this wasn't just a job to my pop. He loves the bridge.

VOCABULARY

A *slatted catwalk* has long, narrow pieces of wood placed closely together to make a walkway.

VOCABULARY

A *swabbie* is a sailor.

VOCABULARY

A *girder* is a heavy beam used to support a building.

In San Francisco there is great excitement. Everyone is waiting for opening day.

Charlie and I have watched nearly every bit of the bridge go up. We saw the two spans come together from opposite directions. We saw them meet. We saw the roadway go in. And my pop did it. No one can be as proud as I am. Not even Charlie. After all, my dad is a skywalker....

On opening day no cars are allowed. Thousands of people walk and dance and roller-skate across the bridge, including us. I wear Pop's kerchief around my neck. There's a man riding a unicycle. There's another on stilts. Navy biplanes fly above the great steel towers. Battleships and cruisers sail below the bridge and into San Francisco Bay. Wind strums its music through the stretch of the cables, and I think of my pop's harp.

That night our family has our own party with Charlie and his dad. There's stewed chicken and a Chinese noodle dish Charlie's dad made and a snickerdoodle pie.

The jigsaw puzzle sits on the coffee table with a gap in the middle. "I've searched and searched for that missing piece," my mother says.

"A good thing we didn't leave our bridge with a space like that," Mr. Shu says.

Pop chuckles. "We'd be working still."

It's time.

I slip upstairs to get the hidden puzzle piece, then find the scissors and cut the piece carefully in half. I go back down and put a half piece in Mr. Shu's hand and the other in my pop's. "Finish it," I say. "It's your bridge. It belongs to both of you."

My mother raises her eyebrows and Charlie says, "Hey, where . . .?" But I just watch as the two pieces fit in, so perfectly, so smoothly.

"Team effort," my pop says.

We raise our glasses of sarsaparilla (sas-puh-RIL-uh) to celebrate the laborers and riveters, the carpenters and the painters and the sky-walkers. All the men who worked together to build the most beautiful bridge in the world.

CULTURAL

Sarsaparilla is a sweet soft drink made from a tropical American plant.

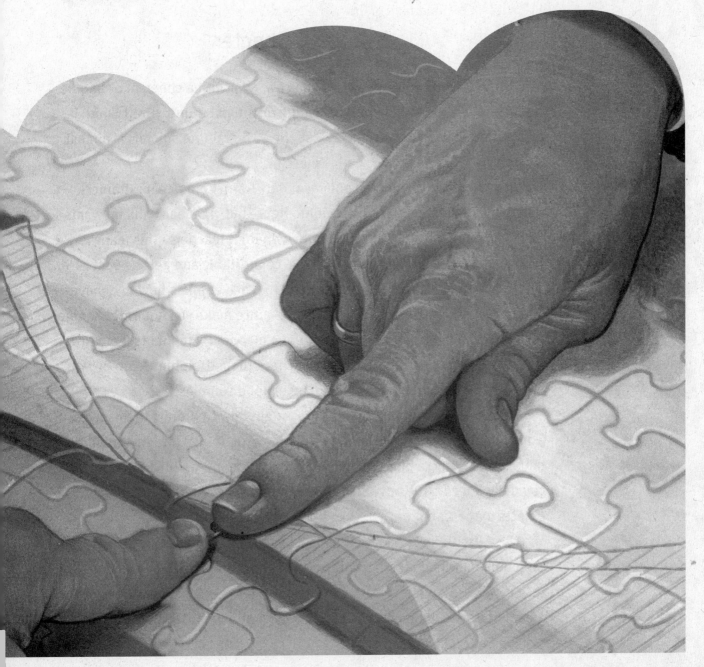

GENRE:
Nonfiction

Animals and Their Trainers
A Good Team

by Sara F. Shacter

Ever wish you could speak to a sparrow, chat with a cheetah, or babble to a baboon? Then think about becoming an animal trainer. Brett Smith is a trainer at Chicago's Lincoln Park Zoo. He says training animals is almost like talking to them.

In a zoo or aquarium, an animal and its trainer are a team. Trainers learn to read their animals' behavior to figure out what each animal wants and needs. Animals learn to cooperate with their teachers. This teamwork makes it possible for each animal to live comfortably and get the best care.

For everyone's safety, trainers need to teach animals how to behave during a checkup. Do visits to the doctor's office make you squirm? Imagine trying to examine a squirming, trumpeting elephant! Elephants learn how to place their feet so veterinarians can check them. Dolphins learn how to place their tails so veterinarians can take blood samples.

VOCABULARY
A *veterinarian* is a doctor for animals.

At some aquariums, dolphins are taught how to protect themselves from humans' mistakes. Sometimes people drop things into the dolphins' tank. In the water, a plastic bag looks a lot like a squid. But a dolphin could die if it eats the bag. So these dolphins are trained to bring stray objects to the trainers.

Because trainers and their animals spend so much time together, their bond of trust is strong. This bond helps trainers do important research. For example, a trainer might be able to get up close when a mother is feeding her new baby. That's something most wild animals wouldn't allow.

Fun and Rewards

How do trainers teach animals? Ken Ramirez is the head trainer at Chicago's John G. Shedd Aquarium. He says that animals and people learn best the same way: through fun and rewards.

Mr. Ramirez doesn't punish. He wants the animals to have a good time. When the animal does what it's supposed to do, it gets a reward. Often the reward is food, but it can be something else. Belugas (white whales), for example, love having their tongues tickled.

Trainers believe that it's also important to give animals the chance to play. New sights, sounds, and experiences keep animals' minds and bodies healthy. At the Shedd Aquarium, dolphins enjoy watching their reflections in mirrors. One dolphin looks at herself for hours. At the Lincoln Park Zoo, lions play with piñatas. The lions rush up, smack their prey, and jump away. Once they're sure the piñatas won't fight back, the lions rip them open. They find the food or bone inside and make shredded paper their new toy.

Training animals takes time and patience, but the rewards are huge. Ken Ramirez says a trainer is an animal's "parent, doctor, playmate, and best friend." Animals may not speak our language, but they have much to tell us.

> **CULTURAL**
> A *piñata* is a Spanish word for a decorated container, filled with toys and candy, that children break open at a party.

Who's Training Whom?

Ken Ramirez once worked with a dolphin that could always find a piece of trash in his tank, even when the pool looked clean. The dolphin earned a fish reward for each piece of trash he turned in.

Soon the trainers became suspicious. They began saving everything the dolphin found, from bags to newspaper scraps. When they noticed that the newspaper scraps fit together, they realized what was going on.

The dolphin had found a little nook in the tank, perfect for storing trash. When he wanted a snack, he'd grab some garbage and turn it in for a treat. Smart dolphin!

WEIRD FRIENDS

UNLIKELY ALLIES IN THE ANIMAL KINGDOM

by Jose Aruego and Ariane Dewey

Sometimes in the wild, animals you might think could hurt each other actually help each other in surprising ways. They share food or a home. They warn one another of approaching predators. They cluster side by side for protection. Some animals even give others a good bath. Their survival often depends on these weird friendships.

The Rhino and the Cattle Egret

As they graze across the plains, a rhino and her calf stir up grass-hoppers. But the rhino can't see very well and may not notice danger approaching. So she lets a sharp-eyed cattle egret (EE-gret) perch on her back to act as a lookout. The egret is rewarded with an endless feast of grasshoppers.

If the egret spies danger, it screams. And if *that* doesn't get the rhino's attention, it taps on the rhino's head until the mother and baby gallop to safety.

The Ostrich and the Zebra

Ostriches have terrific eyes. Zebras have terrific ears. When the two get together, nothing can sneak up on them. That's why ostriches and zebras often roam the savanna together, chomping on seeds and grasses. The ostriches look, and the zebras listen, for predators. The first to detect a hungry lion warns the others, and before it can attack, they all flee to safety.

VOCABULARY
A *savanna* is a flat, grassy area of land where wild animals live.

The Hermit Crab and the Sea Anemones

When a hermit crab needs a new home, it finds an empty shell, moves in, and sticks sea anemones (a-NEM-a-neez) on top for protection. The anemones' stinging tentacles scare away octopuses, which love to eat hermit crabs. Anemones can't walk, so the crab provides them with transportation to new feeding spots. And because crabs are messy eaters, there are always food scraps for the anemones to nibble.

The Impalas and the Baboons

VOCABULARY
Delicate means small and beautiful.

At the water hole, a herd of delicate impalas stays close to a troop of tough baboons. The impalas use their excellent senses of smell, hearing, and sight to detect danger.

If the impalas notice a predator approaching, they dance nervously. That warns the baboons, who bare their fangs and snarl to scare the attacker away.

The Forest Mouse and the Beetles

At night, the forest mouse scampers around the rain forest looking for food, with beetles clinging to its fur and face. But the mouse doesn't mind, because the beetles eat the fleas that infest its fur. During the day, while the mouse sleeps, the beetles dismount and eat the bugs in the mouse's burrow. The beetles are always well fed, and the mouse and its house are free of itchy insects.

VOCABULARY

If fleas *infest* an animal's fur, then a large number of fleas live in the animal's fur.

The Water Thick-Knees and the Crocodile

A bird called a water thick-knees sometimes builds its nest next to a crocodile's home. When the crocodile leaves to go hunting, the bird watches both of their nests.

If trouble threatens the eggs or young in either nest, the bird screeches until the crocodile comes charging home. The water thick-knees and her family are safe beside their ferocious neighbor, because the crocodile will not eat its baby-sitter.

VOCABULARY

A *screech* is a sharp, loud cry.

HOW CAN YOU MAKE GOLD?

by Vicki Cobb

You can't make gold. Plain and simple. But hundreds of years ago, some people believed that you could make gold out of other metals, like iron or copper. So they mixed and stirred and heated all kinds of things. They discovered that the only way to end up with gold was to start with gold. They couldn't make gold from anything else because gold is one of the simplest materials on earth. It is an *element*.

There are ninety-two elements in nature. Maybe you already know some of them. Here are a few examples: silver, oxygen, nitrogen, hydrogen, carbon, iron, and neon. Imagine chopping up an element into smaller and smaller pieces. The smallest piece you can get of an element is an *atom*. Atoms are so incredibly tiny that it's hard to imagine how small they are. If you can imagine how many grains of sand there are on a beach, then

that's how many atoms there are in a single grain of sand! Gold is a very dense element because its atoms are packed close together.

The people who tried to make gold discovered many other elements besides gold. They also learned that elements can come together and form completely new materials. Elements are like the letters of the alphabet, which combine to make words. For example, iron can combine with oxygen in the air to form a red powder. You know this red powder as *rust*. The smallest part of rust is made up of iron and oxygen atoms. Whenever two or more atoms are combined, a *molecule* is formed. Molecules are bigger than atoms, but they are still incredibly small. Rust is made of molecules, and it is not an element. It is called a *compound*.

Elements combine to form compounds in a chemical reaction. For example, hydrogen reacts with oxygen to form water. This reaction is so strong that there is an explosion. Compounds can also react with one another to make different compounds. The science that discovered elements, compounds, and chemical reactions is called *chemistry*.

Goldilocks
and the Three Bears

retold by James Marshall

Once there was a little girl called Goldilocks.

"What a sweet child," said someone new in town.

"That's what *you* think," said a neighbor.

One morning Goldilocks's mother sent her to buy muffins in the next village. "You must promise *not* to take the shortcut through the forest," she said. "I've heard that bears live there."

"I promise," said Goldilocks.

But to tell the truth, Goldilocks was one of those naughty little girls who do *exactly* as they please.

Meanwhile in a clearing deeper inside the forest, in a charming house all their own, a family of brown bears was sitting down to breakfast.

"Patooie!" cried big old Papa Bear. "This porridge is scalding! I've burned my tongue!"

"I'm dying!" cried Baby Bear.

"Now really," said Mama Bear, who was of medium size. "That's quite enough."

"I know," said Papa Bear. "Why don't we go for a spin while the porridge is cooling?"

"Excellent," said Mama Bear.

So they got on their rusty old bicycle and off they went.

A few minutes later, Goldilocks arrived at the bears' house. She walked right in without *even* bothering to knock. On the dining room table were three inviting bowls of porridge.

Tra la!

"I don't mind if I do," said Goldilocks, helping herself to the biggest bowl.

But the porridge in the biggest bowl was much too hot.

"Patooie!" cried Goldilocks.

And she spat it out. Next she tasted the porridge in the medium-sized bowl. But that porridge was much too cold.

Then Goldilocks tasted the porridge in the little bowl, and it was *just right*—neither too hot nor too cold.

In fact, she liked it so much that she gobbled it all up.

Feeling full and satisfied, Goldilocks thought it would be great fun to have a look around. Right away she noticed a lot of coarse brown fur everywhere.

"They must have kitties," she said.

In the parlor there were three chairs.

"I don't mind if I do," she said, climbing into the biggest one. But the biggest chair was much too hard, and she just couldn't get comfortable.

Next she sat in the medium-sized chair. But that chair was much too soft. (And she thought she might *never* get out of it.)

Then Goldilocks sat in the little chair, and that was *just right*—neither too hard nor too soft. In fact, she liked it so much that she rocked and rocked—until the chair fell completely to pieces!

VOCABULARY

If someone is *tuckered out*, he or she is very tired.

Now, all that rocking left Goldilocks quite tuckered out.

"I could take a little snooze," she said.

So she went to look for a comfy place to nap. Upstairs were three beds.

"I don't mind if I do," said Goldilocks.

And she got into the biggest one. But the head of the biggest bed was much too high.

Next she tried the medium-sized bed. But the head of that bed was much too low. Then Goldilocks tried the little bed, and it was *just right*. Soon she was all nice and cozy and sound asleep. She did not hear the bears come home.

The three bears were mighty hungry. But when they went in for breakfast, they could scarcely believe their eyes!

"Somebody has been in my porridge!" said Papa Bear.

"Somebody has been in *my* porridge!" said Mama Bear.

"Somebody has been in my porridge," said Baby Bear. "And eaten it all up!"

In the parlor the three bears were in for another little surprise.

"Somebody has been sitting in my chair!" said Papa Bear.

"Somebody has been sitting in *my* chair!" said Mama Bear.

"Somebody has been sitting in my chair!" said Baby Bear. "And broken it to smithereens!"

The three bears went upstairs on tiptoe (not knowing what they would discover). At first everything seemed fine. But then Papa Bear lay down on his big brass bed.

"Somebody has been lying in my bed!" he cried.

And he was not amused.

"Egads!" cried Mama Bear. "Somebody has been lying in *my* bed!"

"Look!" cried Baby Bear. "Somebody has been lying in my bed. And she's still there!"

"Now see here!" roared Papa Bear.

Goldilocks woke up with a start. And her eyes nearly popped out of her head. But before the bears could demand a proper explanation, Goldilocks was out of bed, out the window, and on her way home.

"Who *was* that little girl?" asked Baby Bear.

"I have no idea," said Mama Bear. "But I hope we never see her again."

And they never did.

> **VOCABULARY**
> *Smithereens* are fragments or very small pieces.

Evie & Margie

by Bernard Waber

Evie and Margie were best friends. They did everything together.
They even dreamed together. They dreamed of becoming actors.

"Someday we'll be famous," said Evie.

"Someday everyone will want our autographs," said Margie.

"We'll change our names," said Evie.

"Mine will be Mariah," said Margie.

"Mine will be Eliza," said Evie.

"And we'll always be best friends," they promised each other.

But then something happened to test their friendship. It began when
Mr. Stanniss, their teacher, announced: "I am happy to tell you that our
class was selected to present this year's play. We'll be doing *Cinderella*,
and next week everyone can try out for parts."

Evie and Margie both decided to try out for the lead role, the part of
Cinderella.

"But deep down I'll want you to get it," said Margie.

"And deep down I'll want you," said Evie.

They began at once to practice for the tryouts.

"Let's work on the part where Cinderella cries when she can't go to
the ball," said Margie. "Crying parts are so *grrreat*. You first."

"All right," said Evie, making a crying face. "Boo-hoo, I want to go to
the ball, too."

"How was that?" said Evie?

"Ummm . . . okay," said Margie.

"Just . . . okay?"

"You could have cried with real tears," said Margie.

"Real tears?" said Evie.

"Watch me," said Margie.

"Boo-hoo," Margie began in a faint, weepy voice, "I want to go to the ball, too."

Suddenly, Margie's eyes filled with tears. Real tears. Gigantic tears. Tears that quickly became enormous puddles spilling and splashing down her cheeks. And then, just as suddenly . . .

she moaned . . .

shook . . .

swooned . . .

and fell, sobbing, on the bed.

"Margie! Margie! Are you all right?" Evie cried out to her.

Margie giggled. "Of course I'm all right. I was acting."

"Wow," said Evie. "How did you do that?"

"Easy," said Margie. "I just remembered something bad that happened to me—something really, really bad. Something so bad, and so sad, just thinking about it made me cry. My cousin Harriet taught me how to do that. She took acting classes at summer camp, you know."

"What bad thing happened?" said Evie.

"It's a secret," said Margie.

"A secret from me?" said Evie.

"Even from you," said Margie. "It has to be a secret. Harriet warned me about that. Keeping it secret is the only way it will work.

"Now you try it," said Margie.

"But nothing bad ever happened to me," said Evie.

"Pretend, then," said Margie. "Pretend something bad happened to you—or someone you care about."

"Oh, no," said Evie.

"It's only pretend," said Margie.

Evie looked at the clock. "I have to go home," she said.

That night, just before bedtime, Evie tried to think of something bad or sad that had happened to her. Little by little something came to her.

She remembered a kindergarten birthday party, and how she cried and cried because they ran out of cupcakes just when it was her turn to take one—her favorite kind, too, with pink and purple sprinkles.

And then she remembered crying even harder when she was offered a carrot stick instead.

"Perfect," thought Evie. "I'll use that."

So Evie squeezed her eyes real tight, and with all her might tried to feel again the sting of missing out on that long-ago, most-yearned-for cupcake.

Evie got all set for tears, but no tears came. She squeezed her eyes again and again. She squeezed and squeezed and squeezed until her face turned purple from squeezing. Still no tears.

Tryouts were held the next day.

Margie was first. Everyone was astonished by her free-flowing tears. Mr. Stanniss even ran for tissues and helped dry her eyes.

"That was so moving, Margie," he said.

Next it was Evie's turn.

Evie decided to give her sad cupcake memory a second chance. She blinked hard to coax tears, but all she got was one measly tear that somehow was lost trickling down her cheek.

"Nice, Evie," said Mr. Stanniss.

"Now here's what we'll do," Mr. Stanniss went on.

"Margie will play Cinderella, and Evie will be her understudy. That means if Margie can't perform in the play, Evie will take her place. Evie will be Cinderella."

"Does it also mean I won't be in the play?" said Evie.

"You'll have enough to do learning Cinderella's lines," said Mr. Stanniss. "So in the play you can be a tree in the forest. As Cinderella runs past, you will say, 'Whoosh!'"

Evie tried hard to feel happy for Margie, but at home she cried and cried. Real tears. Honest tears. Big sloppy tears—bigger, fatter, and wetter tears than Margie's. And bit by bit, sob by sob, gulp by gulp, sniffle by sniffle, she blurted out what had happened—how she ended up playing a tree, and how her only line in the entire play was whoosh!

"Whoosh?" said her mother.

"Whoosh?" said her father.

"Yes, whoosh," cried Evie. "And I don't even feel like a tree," she burst out, with fresh tears.

Her father dried Evie's eyes and let her blow her nose into his handkerchief. And then he said, "Listen, Evie, you're going to go out there and slam that word whoosh right out of the ballpark. You're going to be the best whoosher you can possibly be. You're going to whoosh like nobody has ever whooshed. Do you hear me, Evie? Slugger?"

"I hear you," sobbed Evie, "but I still don't like my part."

So every night Evie practiced her one lonely line.

"Whoosh! Whoosh!" she said in different ways.

"Whoosh! Whoosh!" she said in different voices, with different gestures. *"Whoosh! Whoosh! Whoosh!"*

And every day she rehearsed the Cinderella role with Margie.

At last the big day arrived—the day of the show. That morning Evie awoke feeling that something was wrong. Something just didn't feel right.

Soon she knew what was wrong and what didn't feel right. She was jealous of Margie.

Even worse, and much against her will, she began to imagine all manner of circumstances that would prevent Margie from performing in the play.

Evie was so terrified by her jealousy, she welcomed the ringing of the telephone. It was Margie.

"Guess what?" Margie sobbed. "I can't be in the play. I have the worst cold."

"Oh, no," said Evie. "I feel so bad for you." And Evie meant it. She knew, too painfully, how rotten it felt to be disappointed.

"Good luck playing Cinderella," Margie cried as she hung up.

Evie arrived at school in a daze.

"Quickly," said an anxious Mr. Stanniss, "get into the Cinderella costume."

Soon after, the curtain parted and Evie stepped unsteadily onto the stage. She quickly got hold of herself, and when it was time for the big crying scene, Evie was ready. She cried real tears remembering her bitter disappointment with the tree part. And she cried many more tears for Margie's disappointment. But she cried the most tears because being jealous felt so horrible.

The audience cried with her.

Even Mr. Stanniss cried—possibly from relief.

When the play was over, everyone cheered for Evie.

After school, Evie immediately called Margie.

"I heard you were *grrreat*," said Margie.

"But it should have been you playing Cinderella," said Evie.

"Oh, good news," said Margie. "Mr. Stanniss told my mom the play was so wonderful, they're planning another performance. And this time, when I am well, I will be Cinderella. Isn't that *grrreat!*"

"*Grrreat!*" said Evie. "And I'll gladly play the tree."

"*Whoosh!*" Margie said, kiddingly.

"Margie, I have something terrible to tell you," said Evie. "I was jealous of you, and I'm so ashamed."

Margie was quiet for a moment, and then she said, "I was jealous of you, too, Evie."

"You were? Oh, *grrreat!*" said Evie. "I feel so much better now."

The following week Margie was well enough to play Cinderella. Everyone agreed she was wonderful in the role—especially Evie.

And after that they had an ice cream party to celebrate both performances. Oh, and guess what?

Evie had a cupcake with her ice cream.

And guess what else?

Her favorite kind—

with pink and purple sprinkles.

The Sunset in My Mailbox

by Callie Lorentson

Uh-oh. Julien's letter was here. I could tell by the way the mail carrier dropped it in my hands and fled. Peering down at the pastel pink envelope, I saw the words "PLEASE REFRIGERATE CONTENTS" printed in bold black letters on the back.

This should be interesting, I thought as I slit the envelope and tipped its contents into my hand. Something sticky plopped into my palm.

It was a juice bar. A gooey, purple, sticky, slimy, gorgeous-grape-flavored juice bar that had melted all over my pen pal's letter. I deciphered the letter:

Dear Caitlin,

    This juice bar was so delicious that I wanted to share it with you.
It's gorgeous grape, my favorite flavor. Enjoy.

Hugs and smoochies,

Julien

P.S. Next week I'm sending you breakfast.

As I held the stained juice bar stick, I thought, breakfast?! Oh no. I could already imagine a cheese omelet traveling by mail.

Ever since we became pen pals, Julien has sent me strange things. Once, she sent her sneeze in a jar. ("I have a cold, can you tell?" she wrote.) Then she sent her fingerprint. ("So you'll recognize me in a crowd.") One week she even sent a snowball. Or at least it *had been* a snowball. ("Here's a souvenir from my ski vacation.")

Julien sent me breakfast, all right. Cornflakes. Soggy, milky, grainy, crumbly, limp cornflakes scraped from the bottom of her cereal bowl. I lost my appetite, but I read the letter.

Dear Caitlin,

These cornflakes were so nutritious that I wanted to share this high-fiber, low-sodium, just-three-calories, balanced breakfast with you.

Bon appétit,

Julien

P.S. Next week I'm sending you a sunset.

CULTURAL

Bon appétit is a French expression that means "Have a good meal."

"She's mistaken," I told my mom. "No one can send a sunset, not even Julien. It's impossible."

"I don't know," Mom said. "Julien might find a way. After all, she did send you her sneeze." Mom wrinkled her nose at the memory.

A week later, I waited for the mail carrier. I'd be able to tell from his face if Julien really sent a sunset. But he just popped the letters in our mailbox with a smile and continued on his way.

I checked the mail and found a box with air holes and the words "FRAGILE—THIS SIDE UP" printed in bold black letters on the top. It was from Julien.

I stroked the box with my fingers. It was perfectly dry. I smelled it. It didn't reek. I held my breath and started opening the package. What if sunbeams spring out and hit me in the face like those fake snakes in a can? I thought.

VOCABULARY

To *reek* is to have a very unpleasant odor.

My hands shook as I lifted the last flap and peeked inside. Where in the world was the sunset? All I could find was a letter and a twisty, gray, papery shell. It looked like a submarine. I read the letter.

Dear Caitlin,

The sunsets at my house are so beautiful that I had to give you a piece. I counted at least five different colors in one yesterday. Can you find more?

Hugs and smoochies,

Julien

I looked again at the gray shell. That's no sunset, I thought.

"You must mean the *submarines* at your house, Julien," I said. Without reading the postscript, I laid the letter and the submarine on the kitchen table. Then I left the room to find a pen so that I could cross out "sunset" and write "submarine" above it.

When I returned, I stared in shock at the submarine. A creature was oozing out of it! Was it a sea monster? I looked closer. It was a winged creature . . . an insect . . . a butterfly. An orange, blue, purple, red, and gold butterfly. It looked like . . . a sunset!

While the sunset opened and closed its wings to dry them, I read Julien's postscript. It said, "P.S. Next week I'm sending you Japan."

Uh-oh.

THE MONEY TREE

by Sarah Stewart

In January, when Miss McGillicuddy was making a quilt in front of the fire, she noticed an unusual shape outside her living-room window.

In February, as Miss McGillicuddy was looking up from her book, she realized that the new shape was a small tree. "A gift from the birds," she said to herself.

In March, while Miss McGillicuddy was flying her favorite kite, its tail got caught in a limb of the new tree. "What a strange shape," she thought as she tugged.

In April, when Miss McGillicuddy was planting snow peas, she paused and stared at the tree, now covered in the fresh green colors of spring. "How odd," she mused, "that it has grown so very large in such a short time."

In May, as Miss McGillicuddy was making a Maypole for the neighborhood children, she realized, to her great surprise, that the leaves on the tree were not leaf-shaped at all! Being careful not to hurt the tender branches, she gave each child some of the tree's crisp green foliage as a party favor.

CULTURAL
A *maypole* is a pole that is decorated with streamers and flowers to celebrate May Day.

VOCABULARY
Foliage is a covering of leaves, especially as found on a tree.

In June, while Miss McGillicuddy was gathering a bouquet of roses, parents of the neighborhood children appeared in the yard. When they said they had come to see the strange tree, she invited them to take home a few cuttings.

In July, when Miss McGillicuddy was picking cherries in her orchard, the town officials asked if they could use some of the greenery for special projects. She let them borrow her ladder—the tree was growing larger every day—and went inside to make cherry cobbler.

In August, as Miss McGillicuddy was returning home, she noticed that most of the people carrying bags and baskets away from the tree were perfect strangers! "No matter," she said, "the branches would break from their burden if someone was not picking all the time."

In September, while Miss McGillicuddy was feeding the animals, she watched the crowd around the tree surging back and forth beneath the harvest moon. "Don't they ever rest?" she asked herself.

In October, when Miss McGillicuddy was making faces on her pumpkins, she realized that the leaves on the tree were turning yellow and brown. She sighed with relief.

In November, as the first winter storm arrived, Miss McGillicuddy watched a few determined strangers scratching at the snow under the tree.

In December, Miss McGillicuddy and the neighbor boys cut down the tree. Although the wood was green and certain to smoke a little, she didn't mind, for now she had enough to keep warm through the coldest winter.

Miss McGillicuddy gave each boy a loaf of homemade bread, a jar of strawberry jam, and a bouquet of dried flowers. Then she said goodbye, walked toward the warmth of the fire, and smiled to herself.

> **VOCABULARY**
> A *bouquet* is a group of flowers.

A LOG'S LIFE

by Wendy Pfeffer

Deep in a forest a great oak tree stands.

A family of squirrels lives in a hole in its trunk. A porcupine chews on its branches. A colony of carpenter ants nests under the outer bark.

A woodpecker pecks at the rough bark, searching for insects. He spears one, devours it, and hunts for more.

Wood-boring beetles burrow under the bark, chewing wood and leaving tunnels. Water and air seep into the tunnels. Toadstools and other fungi such as mildew, molds, and mushrooms sprout in these damp places. Slugs and snails crawl up the tree trunk into the tunnels and eat the fungi.

One stormy day a strong wind whips through the forest. The old oak bends with every gust. Rain pelts its branches. Wind tosses its leaves through the air. Lightning flashes and sizzles down its trunk.

A thunderous crack startles the porcupine sleeping nearby. The tall oak begins to topple. Squirrels feel the trembling and scramble out of their hole. One strong gust of blustery wind tears the great oak's roots from the ground. The tree crashes down, shaking the forest floor. Branches break. Limbs splinter. Leaves scatter.

Now it's a giant log.

Soon the storm stops and the sun comes out. An umbrella of leaves and tangled branches block the sunshine from the forest floor. The porcupine comes out of its den. Squirrels scamper to see the old hole that was once their home.

Under the log, ants rush about, carrying white bundles of babies. A spider crawls through cracks and crevices, searching for a dry spot to place her egg sac. Millipedes settle between the log and the wet ground. For now, they are safe from the spider. Termites soon discover the fallen log and move in. They not only eat the rotting wood, they lay their eggs there, too.

VOCABULARY

A *crevice* is a very small opening.

For three or four years, through hot, cold, wet and dry seasons, ants, beetles, fungi, slugs, snails, spiders, millipedes, and termites live in the log.

One winter the porcupine's hollow log collapses. He moves into the oak log, too.

In the spring, click beetles snap and click their bodies and flip high in the air before settling in the log. Salamanders, frightened by the noise and sudden movements, dart under the log for safety . . . and stay.

In the summer, pill bugs and slugs crawl inside the cool, moist log to keep from drying out. Pill bugs eat dead leaves. Salamanders eat the pill bugs. Slugs slip out at night and eat almost anything.

The old log provides both food and shelter for the millipedes. They eat decaying plants and trees. But spiders eat the millipedes.

Several more years of hot, cold, wet, and dry seasons pass. Time, weather, and the chewing, pecking, boring, and tunneling of many animals and insects make the inside of the log spongy. The outer bark becomes soft and damp, and gradually it falls to the ground.

VOCABULARY
If a plant is *decaying*, it is rotting.

Wood-boring insects have no wood to bore. They find another log. The woodpecker hunts for other trees to peck. Spiders spin their webs in drier spots. And the porcupine moves to a more solid log.

Slowly, a lush green blanket of moss carpets the rotting log. Its thick roots break down the wood. Over the next few years the log crumbles. What is left looks like dirt. It feels like dirt. It smells like dirt. It *is* dirt.

Earthworms move in. They turn the soil over just as a shovel does. They burrow down and break up the soil just as a rake does. In about ten years the rotting log has become a mound of rich, black earth.

One autumn day an acorn falls from a nearby oak tree. A squirrel buries it in the rich soil. A seedling oak sprouts . . . and grows . . . and grows until . . . one day deep in the forest another great oak tree stands.

Squirrels move in. So do carpenter ants, beetles, and woodpeckers. The ants build nests. The beetles burrow. The woodpeckers peck. For years life goes on in the oak tree.

Then one night the wind whistles through the trees. The old oak bends and shakes. It crashes to the forest floor.

And becomes another giant log.

THUNDER cake

by Patricia Polacco

On sultry summer days at my grandma's farm in Michigan, the air gets damp and heavy. Stormclouds drift low over the fields. Birds fly close to the ground. The clouds glow for an instant with a sharp, crackling light, and then a roaring, low, tumbling sound of thunder makes the windows shudder in their panes. The sound used to scare me when I was little. I loved to go to Grandma's house (Babushka, as I used to call my grandma, had come from Russia years before), but I feared Michigan's summer storms. I feared the sound of thunder more than anything. I always hid under the bed when the storm moved near the farmhouse.

This is the story of how my grandma—my Babushka—helped me overcome my fear of thunderstorms.

Grandma looked at the horizon, drew a deep breath and said, "This is Thunder Cake baking weather, all right. Looks like a storm coming to me."

"Child, you come out from under that bed. It's only thunder you're hearing," my grandma said.

The air was hot, heavy and damp. A loud clap of thunder shook the house, rattled the windows and made me grab her close.

"Steady, child," she cooed. "Unless you let go of me, we won't be able to make a Thunder Cake today!"

"Thunder Cake?" I stammered as I hugged her even closer.

"Don't pay attention to that old thunder, except to see how close the storm is getting. When you see the lightning, start counting . . . real slow. When you hear the thunder, stop counting. That number is how many miles away the storm is. Understand?" she asked. "We need to know how far away the storm is, so we have time to make the cake and get it into the oven before the storm comes, or it won't be real Thunder Cake."

Her eyes surveyed the black clouds a way off in the distance. Then she strode into the kitchen. Her worn hands pulled a thick book from the shelf above the woodstove.

"Let's find that recipe, child," she crowed as she lovingly fingered the grease-stained pages to a creased spot.

"Here it is . . . Thunder Cake!"

She carefully penned the ingredients on a piece of notepaper. "Now let's gather all the things we'll need!" she exclaimed as she scurried toward the back door.

We were by the barn door when a huge bolt of lightning flashed. I started counting, like Grandma told me to, "1-2-3-4-5-6-7-8-9-10."

Then the thunder ROARED!

"Ten miles . . . it's ten miles away," Grandma said as she looked at the sky. "About an hour away, I'd say. You'll have to hurry, child. Gather them eggs careful-like," she said.

Eggs from mean old Nellie Peck Hen. I was scared. I knew she would try to peck me.

"I'm here, she won't hurt you. Just get them eggs," Grandma said softly.

The lightning flashed again. "1-2-3-4-5-6-7-8-9" I counted.

"Nine miles," Grandma reminded me.

Milk was next. Milk from old Kick Cow. As Grandma milked her, Kick Cow turned and looked mean, right at me. I was scared. She looked so big.

ZIP went the lightning. "1-2-3-4-5-6-7-8" I counted.

BAROOOOOOOOM went the thunder.

"Eight miles, child," Grandma croaked. "Now we have to get chocolate and sugar and flour from the dry shed."

I was scared as we walked down the path from the farmhouse through Tangleweed Woods to the dry shed. Suddenly the lightning slit the sky!

"1-2-3-4-5-6-7" I counted.

BOOOOOOM BA-BOOOOOOM, crashed the thunder. It scared me a lot, but I kept walking with Grandma.

Another jagged edge of lightning flashed as I crept into the dry shed! "1-2-3-4-5-6" I counted.

CRACKLE, CRACKLE BOOOOOOOOM, KA-BOOOOOM, the thunder bellowed. It was dark and I was scared.

"I'm here, child," Grandma said softly from the doorway. "Hurry now, we haven't got much time. We've got everything but the secret ingredient."

"Three overripe tomatoes and some strawberries," Grandma whispered as she squinted at the list.

I climbed up high on the trellis. The ground looked a long way down. I was scared.

"I'm here, child," she said. Her voice was steady and soft. "You won't fall."

I reached three luscious tomatoes while she picked strawberries. Lightning again!

"1-2-3-4-5" I counted.

KA-BANG BOOOOOOOOOAROOOOM, the thunder growled.

We hurried back to the house and the warm kitchen, and we measured the ingredients. I poured them into the mixing bowl while Grandma mixed. I churned butter for the frosting and melted chocolate. Finally, we poured the batter into the cake pans and put them into the oven together.

Lightning lit the kitchen. I only counted to three and the thunder RRRRUMBLED and CRASHED.

"Three miles away," Grandma said, "and the cake is in the oven. We made it! We'll have a real Thunder Cake!"

As we waited for the cake, Grandma looked out the window for a long time. "Why, you aren't afraid of thunder. You're too brave!" she said as she looked right at me.

"I'm not brave, Grandma," I said. "I was under the bed! Remember?"

"But you got out from under it," she answered, "and you got eggs from mean old Nellie Peck Hen, you got milk from old Kick Cow, you went through Tangleweed Woods to the dry shed, you climbed the trellis in the barnyard. From where I sit, only a very brave person could have done all them things!"

I thought and thought as the storm rumbled closer. She was right. I was brave!

"Brave people can't be afraid of a sound, child," she said as we spread out the tablecloth and set the table. When we were done, we hurried into the kitchen to take the cake out of the oven. After the cake had cooled, we frosted it.

Just then the lightning flashed, and this time it lit the whole sky.

Even before the last flash had faded, the thunder ROLLED, BOOOOOMED, CRASHED, and BBBBAAAARRRRR-OOOOOOOOMMMMMM-MMMMED just above us. The storm was here!

"Perfect," Grandma cooed, "just perfect." She beamed as she added the last strawberry to the glistening chocolate frosting on top of our Thunder Cake.

As rain poured down on our roof, Grandma cut a wedge for each of us. She poured us steaming cups of tea from the samovar.

When the thunder ROARED above us so hard it shook the windows and rattled the dishes in the cupboards, we just smiled and ate our Thunder Cake.

From that time on, I never feared the voice of thunder again.

CULTURAL

Samovar is a Russian word for a metal container with a faucet and heater that is used to boil or warm tea.

Red Riding Hood

retold by James Marshall

A long time ago in a simple cottage beside the deep, dark woods, there lived a pretty child called Red Riding Hood. She was kind and **considerate**, and everybody loved her.

One afternoon Red Riding Hood's mother called to her. "Granny isn't feeling up to snuff today," she said, "so I've baked her favorite custard as a little surprise. Be a good girl and take it to her, will you?"

Red Riding Hood was delighted. She loved going to Granny's—even though it meant crossing the deep, dark woods.

When the custard had cooled, Red Riding Hood's mother wrapped it up and put it in a basket.

"Now, whatever you do," she said, "go straight to Granny's, do not tarry, do not speak to any strangers."

"Yes, Mama," said Red Riding Hood.

Before long she was in the deepest part of the woods.

"Oooh," she said. "This is scary."

Suddenly a large wolf appeared.

"Good afternoon, my dear," he said. "Care to stop for a little chat?"

"Oh, gracious me," said Red Riding Hood. "Mama said not to speak to any strangers."

But the wolf had *such* charming manners.

"And where are you going, sweet thing?" he said.

"I'm on my way to visit Granny, who lives in the pretty yellow house on the other side of the woods," said Red Riding Hood. "She's feeling poorly, and I'm taking her a surprise."

"You don't say," said the wolf. Just then he had a delightful idea. No reason why I can't eat them *both*, he thought. "Allow me to escort you," he said. "You never know what might be lurking about."

"You're too kind," said Red Riding Hood.

Beyond the forest they came to a patch of sunflowers.

"Why not pick a few?" suggested the wolf. "Grannies *love* flowers, you know."

But while Red Riding Hood was picking a pretty bouquet, the clever wolf hurried on ahead to Granny's house.

"Who is it?" called out Granny.

"It is I, your delicious—er—darling granddaughter," said the wolf in a high voice.

"The door is unlocked," said Granny.

"Surprise!" cried the wolf.

Granny was furious at having her reading interrupted.

"Get out of here, you horrid thing!" she cried.

But the wolf gobbled her right up. He didn't even bother to chew.

"Tasty," he said, patting his belly, "so tasty."

Just then he heard footsteps on the garden path.

"Here comes dessert!"

And losing no time, he put on Granny's cap and glasses, jumped into bed, and pulled up the covers.

"Who is it?" he called out in his sweetest granny voice.

"It is I, your little granddaughter," said Red Riding Hood.

"The door is unlocked," said the wolf.

Red Riding Hood was distressed at seeing her grandmother so changed.

VOCABULARY
To be *distressed*, is to be worried or upset.

"Why, Granny," she said, "what big eyes you have."

"The better to see you, my dear," said the wolf.

"And Granny, what long arms you have."

"The better to hug you, my dear," said the wolf.

"And Granny, what big teeth you have."

"THE BETTER TO EAT YOU, MY DEAR!" cried the wolf.

And he gobbled her right up. "I'm so wicked," he said. "*So* wicked."

But really he was enormously pleased with himself. And having enjoyed such a heavy meal, he was soon snoring away.

A hunter passing by was alarmed by the frightful racket.

"That doesn't sound like Granny!" he said.

And so the brave hunter jumped in the window, did in the sleeping wolf, and opened him up. Out jumped Granny and Red Riding Hood.

"We're ever so grateful," said Red Riding Hood.

"That wicked wolf won't trouble you again," said the hunter.

"It was so dark in there I couldn't read a *word*," said Granny.

Red Riding Hood promised never, *ever* to speak to another stranger, charming manners or not.

And she never did.

Storytelling Trees

by Micki Huysken

Cedar trees grow in the Alaskan forest. A Tlingit (CLING-it) Indian walks among them searching for the right one. He finds a strong, straight tree that has been growing long before his grandfather's grandfather lived there. He marks its rough bark. This is the first step in making a magnificent storytelling tree.

Long ago, before writing was used by Indians, totem poles were carved to tell stories or to record events happening in the tribe.

Shapes of bears, wolves, whales, eagles, and other wild creatures were carved into soft, tree trunks. The tree was read from top to bottom by a storyteller. Stories often included animals with superhuman powers and stories about the Eagle and Raven clans. These totem poles were read again and again like a library of wooden stories.

Have you seen pictures of totem poles or visited the state of Alaska or Washington where poles stand? Even today, totem-pole carving continues in Ketchikan, Alaska, where Tlingit Indians still live.

Once, a stone adze (an ax-like tool) brought down an 80-foot giant. Today, chain saws do the work in less time.

Thick bark is stripped away; then knots, once burned with hot rocks, are sanded smooth. At last, the tree is ready for the master carver chosen by the tribe. Poles that once took a year to carve can be completed in three months.

The carver chants to help his concentration and to keep a cutting rhythm. It is a chant he learned from his father who learned it from his. Wood chips pepper the air. Animals with beaver tails, whales, wolves, and birds with oversized beaks are chiseled into the soft wood. Some carvings have human shapes.

Long ago, artists mixed salmon eggs with minerals like hematite, graphite, and copper to make bright-colored paints for the poles.

At last, the weary carver puts down his tools. He is ready for a crane to lift the new pole. He thinks back and remembers stories of his grandfather's first pole raising. That one took place at the river's edge. No crane was used then, just dozens of men holding tightly to ropes. Their groans rippled like a chorus of bears; sweat beaded on their backs. Drums and voices swelled like thunder when the pole rose.

The old carver blinks away the memories as a ray of sun touches his sensitive eyes. The steel arm crane is placing his new pole upright facing the road. Arriving visitors look up in awe. Cheers and laughter roll forth like water from a bubbling pot. What was once a mighty cedar growing tall in the Alaskan forest is now a magnificent totem pole.

Think about stories told by your parents and grandparents. If you put those stories on a totem pole, what would your storytelling tree look like?

CULTURAL
Encourage students to share stories about their family heritage.

Building Liberty

by Susan Yoder Ackerman

October 28, 1876   Paris

Dear Cousin Philip,

Happy 100th Birthday! Of course, I know you're only eight like me. But Papa says that now your country, the United States, has had its freedom for a whole century.

Did you know that French children like me, and grownups, too, are giving money to make a birthday gift for your country? It's being made right here in Paris by Papa's friend Mr. Bartholdi. He is making a gigantic sculpture to remind people of liberty.

Papa says it will be the tallest statue in the world. But it will take a long time to finish.

> Your cousin,
> Colette Gaget

June 14, 1878   Paris

Dear Cousin Philip,

You asked so many questions in your last letter! I guess now that Mr. Bartholdi is building his statue in Papa's workshop, you think I know everything. Well, I'll tell you what I can.

First, Mr. Bartholdi took clay and made a four-foot-high model of a lady. He made a torch of freedom for her to carry. He made her walking away from broken chains. She carries a tablet with the date of American independence on it: July 4, 1776. And her crown will have seven rays to represent the seven seas and the seven continents of the world.

When Mr. Bartholdi was happy with his small statue, he made bigger and bigger copies out of plaster until he had one 38 feet tall. It was so large—Papa built a special shed in the workyard to hold it. But it was only one-quarter of the size Mr. Bartholdi wants the statue to be when it is finally done.

You will not believe what they did next. They cut the plaster model into big slices! That's because they can't build a full-size model of the statue in one piece—it would be too big. So they have to make one section at a time, instead. They take each slice and measure very carefully, over and over, in order to make a full-size copy.

There's so much to do. Papa has 50 men working on it every day!

Your cousin,
Colette Gaget

January 5, 1880   Paris

Dear Cousin Philip,

   These days there's hardly room for the cat to walk through Papa's shop! There are layers of the Statue of Liberty everywhere! Each layer is about 30 feet wide and 12 feet high—as big as a house! You asked me if the finished statue will be made of plaster. Oh, no! It's going to be made of thin copper. To get the copper the right shape, wooden molds made of lots and lots of boards are built using the plaster model. Then, when sheets of copper are hammered into the wooden molds, they will be exactly the same shape as the model! It's so clever. Papa's workmen will then bolt and rivet the sheets of copper together to make the statue.

   But there was a big problem. Mr. Bartholdi didn't know how he was going to make the thin copper strong enough so that the statue wouldn't bend or blow over in the wind. He thought of filling the statue with sand or stones, but it is much too big.

   Luckily he talked to Mr. Eiffel, the man who builds bridges. Some people call him the Magician of Iron. Mr. Eiffel had the great idea of making a wrought-iron skeleton inside the statue to hold it up.

                                          Your cousin,
                                          Colette Gaget

August 20, 1884   Paris

Dear Cousin Philip,

   The statue is finished! She towers over the buildings of Paris.

   On July 4th Mr. Bartholdi proudly led American officials up the spiral staircase inside the statue to her crown. The view of the city from there is wonderful!

I often stand by the workyard gate to take money from people who want to see her before she goes to America. Her reddish copper color will become a dull green in time, but I think she will always be beautiful.

I'm glad the Americans don't have the money yet to finish building the pedestal where she will stand. I will miss her when she goes to her island in New York. I can't remember Papa's shop without the statue.

Your cousin,
Colette Gaget

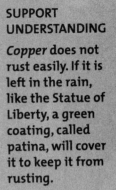

SUPPORT UNDERSTANDING

Copper does not rust easily. If it is left in the rain, like the Statue of Liberty, a green coating, called patina, will cover it to keep it from rusting.

March 30, 1885   Paris

Dear Cousin Philip,

Mr. Bartholdi has lost his patience. He is taking the statue apart and packing it up. He wants to see it standing in New York Harbor. Coming, ready or not!

Each piece is carefully marked before it is packed. I hope it won't be too hard for the Americans to figure out how to put the puzzle together! There are more than 200 huge crates.

I'm glad that the American schoolchildren are sending their pennies to help pay for the huge pedestal the Statue of Liberty needs to stand on. It's so nice that they like the gift the French are giving them.

And here's another gift just for you. When the ship arrives in New York in June, with all the pieces of the Statue of Liberty, I will be waving from the deck. Look for me; I'm all grown up!

Till then,
Colette Gaget

LUCK

by Jean Craighead George

A young sandhill crane spread his six-foot wings and flew away.

"Good-bye, Luck!" called the girl who had set him free.

"That's not his name," said a bird-watcher. "In Asia, where I come from, a crane is called Love."

"Love is a beautiful name," said the girl, "but any bird that sticks its head in a plastic six-pack holder is going to need more luck than love."

Once freed, Luck trilled to his parents. *Crackaarr!*

CRACKAARR! his parents trumpeted from the sky. The young crane spiraled up to meet them. Together they circled the Texas marsh.

It was March. Luck's parents were preparing for their long migration north to their nesting grounds. They were memorizing the reeds and waters of their winter home for their return in autumn. But Luck was memorizing the blue sunglasses on the face of the girl who had saved his life. To Luck she had become home.

Luck and his parents soared across the Texas border, memorizing the hills and rivers below. Above Cherokee, Oklahoma, hundreds of cranes from Mexico joined them.

Luck circled a windmill.

By the time he had it memorized, his parents were far ahead.

Crackaarr, crackaarr, Luck trilled over and over.

CRACKAARR, CRACKAARR. His parents' voices! Their red crowns caught his eye. Luck caught up with them over a shopping mall in Kansas. His parents memorized the cornfields around the mall. Luck memorized a baby carriage.

Ten thousand more cranes joined Luck and his parents above the wetlands of Cheyenne Bottoms in Kansas. They came from Mexico, Louisiana, Nevada, and Arizona. Some had flown in from Florida. There were young cranes like Luck, with no red caps, and old cranes, all headed north. They formed a ten-mile line, three miles wide.

Luck looked down on Route 70 in Kansas and memorized a pack of motorcycles. Suddenly a storm struck, and the cranes were blown far off course. When the storm was over, Luck memorized a boy in a canoe on the Little Blue River.

> **VOCABULARY**
> A *course* is a set path of travel.

The old cranes steered the young back to Route 183 in northern Kansas and then on to Nebraska. In the distance, like a star on the horizon, the Platte River shone silver-gold. When Luck saw the river, he called out, *Crackaarr!*

And five hundred thousand cranes joined in, their voices like wind trumpets, swelling to a choir and then to a symphony.

The children in the school yards in Kearney, Nebraska, heard the symphony and stopped playing games. "Here come the cranes!" they shouted. "Spring is here!"

Farmers heard the ancient voices and readied their tractors for plowing. Bird-watchers saw them and cheered. Photographers snapped pictures.

Luck soared, dipped, and glided. He made designs in the sky with the other cranes. Somehow he remembered the river, although he had never been there before. It was an old memory—about twenty million years old.

Luck let down his long legs, cupped his wings, bowed his tail, and gracefully parachuted into the waters of the Platte River.

Crackaarr, Luck called.

HKKKKKKKKKK, trumpeted the cranes around him. He heard no *CRACKAARR*s from his parents.

Crackaarr, he called again.

HKKKKKKKKKK.

Luck was lost. He waded slowly and deliberately into the shallow river, then stood still. Thousands of cranes gathered around him, trumpeting and flapping. The sun set. Night came. Luck called for his parents once more. No answer. Tired from his long flight, he tucked his beak into his back feathers, stood on one leg, and slept.

The sun came up. The cranes flew and came down in a cornfield.

Luck was hungry. He fed on fallen kernels of corn and soybeans from last autumn's harvest. He chased bugs and ate them.

At dusk Luck and the thousands of cranes flew back to the spot where he had slept. Luck's space was taken by two *HKKKKKKKKKK*ers. Their wings hit him. Their beaks struck at him. He jumped up, spread his wings, and hung above the cranes like a kite. Then a gentle wind carried him upriver.

CRACKAARR. Luck's voice was changing. It was deep. Would his parents recognize his new voice?

CRACKAARR. They knew him! Luck parachuted down. His parents jumped in the air. Throwing back their heads, they all danced for joy.

For almost two weeks Luck and his parents and five hundred thousand other cranes flew from the river to the fields, and from the fields to the river. Then they were gone.

The children went back to their games.

By the time the farmers were tilling the soil, Luck and all the sandhill cranes were far north. A few went to Wyoming and on west. Others winged north into Canada—some went to Manitoba and Saskatchewan. Some flew on to Hudson Bay. Luck and his parents went straight up the Rocky Mountain chain to Alaska. There were no roads with malls and baby carriages, so Luck memorized the snowcapped mountains of the Brooks Range.

The three cranes flew into a dense fog over the Bering Strait. They followed the angle of the sun's rays, as their ancestors had done. Luck memorized the sound of foghorns on ships.

In Siberia Luck was back where he had been born!

His parents started a new family. Luck flew west. He winged over a marsh. Below, a female crane was calling for a mate. Luck parachuted to her side. He bowed. She bowed back. It was June. By the end of the summer they were a pair. Her name was Wise. Luck and Wise danced and composed their own song.

KHARRRR.

KHARRRR. This song would keep them together for as long as they lived.

In late August Luck and Wise flew back across the Bering Strait. Luck heard no foghorns. He was lost. Wise was not. She recalled the angle of the sun's rays and bugled, *KHARRRR.* Luck followed the song.

When they came to the snow-covered Alaskan peaks, Luck brought them down into the tundra wetlands to sleep. By day he led them across Canada and then the Dakotas.

Then Luck saw the Platte River, but it was sleeping until spring. Luck and Wise kept flying south.

Over Kansas Luck turned east to find the boy and the canoe. Wise did not follow. She came down to rest in the reeds in the Cheyenne Bottoms.

KHARRRR, Luck called for her. No answer. He was lost again. He flew west looking for a baby carriage. But no baby carriage was to be found.

Above Route 70 a flock of motorcycles appeared. He remembered and followed them to Route 183 and on to Route 283.

There stood the windmill. Now he truly knew where he was, and he flew straight to the Texas marsh and looked for his "home," the girl with the blue glasses who had saved his life. She was not there. He kept flying.

A plastic six-pack holder glistened in the reeds below. Luck flew to it. The bird-watcher was on the boardwalk. Beside him stood the girl. She was not wearing her blue sunglasses.

"No! No! No!" the girl shouted, and waded into the water. She frightened Luck. He flapped to a grassy slope and landed, pointing his beak skyward.

KHARRRR. Wise dropped down beside him. They lifted their wings and leaped high in the air.

VOCABULARY

A *tundra* is a large area of land covered with snow, but containing no trees.

The girl picked up the plastic six-pack holder and smiled as the cranes danced.

"Luck," she called to the graceful bird, "I've just changed your name to Love."

KHARRRR.

KHARRRR.

The cranes told her their real names and went on dancing.

The Tragic Night

by Kalli Dakos

Bloom! Bloom!
I was supposed to bloom
When the lights shone
On my side of the room!

I was a tulip,
In our class spring play,
My part was to bloom,
When lights shone my way.

All of the flowers
Were curled up so tight,
On one side of the stage,
In the dark of the night.

Bloom! Bloom!
I was supposed to bloom
When the lights shone
On my side of the room!

I waited
For those lights to say,
Flowers, bloom,
It's a splendid day!

I didn't open my eyes
Or even take a glimpse,
But it took so long that
My whole body grew limp.

Bloom! Bloom!
I was supposed to bloom
When the lights shone
On my side of the room!

I started to hear
Such a soft, dreamy tune,
Then I fell asleep,
In my flower costume.

And that's when the lights shone
On my side of the room.

All the tulips
So slowly rose,
Stretched their petals,
Began to grow,
Filled a garden
In perfect rows.

But

One dumb flower
Stayed tucked up tight,
Didn't hear the sounds,
Didn't see the lights,
Didn't bloom at all,
That tragic night.

Bloom! Bloom!
I was supposed to bloom
When the lights shone
On my side of the room!

> **VOCABULARY**
> *Tragic* means "very sad."

LIVING AT THE BOTTOM OF THE WORLD

by David Krakowski as told to Jessica Perez

Where Was I?

Palmer Station is on Anvers Island, 20 miles west of the Antarctic Peninsula. To get there, I sailed from the southern tip of Chile on the Research Vessel Ice Breaker *Nathaniel B. Palmer* for four days on rough seas and through thick sea ice.

Why Did I Go There?

I was in Antarctica to study invertebrates (animals without backbones), such as sea stars and sea urchins. I worked with the divers to collect invertebrates and to set up experiments—and I helped them with their equipment. Sometimes the divers found interesting animals to show everyone—like giant sea cockroaches!

Because the weather outside was very cold and windy, I wore special clothing issued by the U.S. Antarctic Program—socks, boots, a hat, a waterproof coat, and gloves. Anytime I was near the water, I wore a bright-orange float-coat that worked as a life preserver. The divers wore even more warm layers plus a watertight dry suit to protect them from the icy water. They also carried more than 50 pounds of equipment.

Inside the station, I worked in the indoor aquarium and the laboratories, examining specimens through a microscope. I wore clothes just like yours. Palmer Station was kept well heated and protected from the weather outside.

Food and Water

You might think that the food at a polar station would be gross. You'd be wrong. We had two cooks who made delicious meals every day. At Palmer Station, fresh water was precious. Melting glacier ice for water used a lot of fuel, so we purified the salty seawater. We conserved fresh water whenever possible.

VOCABULARY
A *glacier* is a large mass of ice moving slowly over land.

Exploring

On weekends, we hiked or skied on the glacier behind the station or took short boat trips. To be able to explore or work "off-station," everyone first went to Survival School—a safety and survival training class.

When we were on the glacier, we stayed on marked paths to avoid falling into deep cracks in the ice hidden by snow. On boat trips, we avoided dangerous icebergs. We were careful not to disturb any animals, because there are strict rules to protect them. A few times, penguins and seals visited us at the station, though.

Evening Activities

After a long day of work or play, we relaxed. Everyone ate dinner together in the cafeteria. Then, I'd head to the game room. We watched movies on a big-screen TV, played computer games, and even had parties. No TV or radio stations come into Antarctica, so we communicated with the outside world using e-mail. We got regular mail, but it took about a month for it to get to the station in good weather.

Because I woke every day at 7:00 A.M. (in spring, this was four or five hours after sunrise), I was exhausted by 11:00 P.M. You need a good night's sleep to be ready for another exciting day on Palmer Station!

THEY ONLY COME OUT AT NIGHT

by Sneed B. Collard III

Most of us have seen pictures or movies of tropical rain forests. We know they are bursting with birds, jaguars, monkeys, insects, and lots of other creatures. If you ever visit a rain forest, however, you may find yourself asking, "Where are all the animals?"

Most of them are hiding!

Different animals hide in different ways. Some use camouflage to blend in with their surroundings. Other animals are nocturnal. They hide during the daytime and only come out at night.

VOCABULARY
Camouflage is a covering or a way to hide something.

I once visited a tropical rain forest atop a mountain in Costa Rica. During the day, I hiked through the forest and saw hundreds of marvelous rain forest plants. I also spotted beautiful birds, a few butterflies, and even a monkey or two. But to see more, I decided I'd have to act like a rain forest animal myself and come out at night.

An hour after sunset, several other visitors and I followed a guide into the forest. Equipped with flashlights, we began walking down a trail. All around us, the trees rose into the dark sky like silent sentries. Overhead, clouds blanketed the stars, wiping out all traces of light.

VOCABULARY
A *sentry* is a guard.

The forest was much noisier now than in the daytime. Insect and frog voices hummed and buzzed and croaked all around me. Water from the damp, tropical air rolled off leaves and dripped, dripped, dripped onto the rain forest floor.

But the biggest surprise was yet to come. When I shone my flashlight on the nearby trees and shrubs, I found hundreds of eyes shining back at me! These watchful eyes belonged to insects, lizards, frogs, spiders, and other small forest creatures. It seemed that I had stumbled onto an all-night animal party.

Most amazing of all were the insects—especially the walking sticks. They're among the longest insects on earth, and in Southeast Asia they can grow up to thirteen inches long. The ones I saw were about as long as a pencil and looked almost exactly like twigs. The walking sticks were a little scary at first, until I learned that they munch on leaves and other plant material—not tourists.

Another fascinating group of insects was the katydids. They made high, whining calls and had surprising shapes. Some resembled grass-hoppers, while others looked like leaves with legs. (I guess nocturnal animals can use camouflage, too.)

VOCABULARY
To *flit* is to fly quickly.

Moths of all kinds sat on branches or flitted about us. Their wings ranged from bright orange to the gray-blue of a tree trunk. Lots and lots of bats flitted about, too.

Why are so many animals nocturnal? Coming out only at night has its advantages. In the desert, for instance, hot daytime temperatures force many creatures to stay in burrows or under rocks until the cool of night arrives. While high temperatures aren't usually a problem in a shady rain forest, getting eaten is. We often think of tropical rain forests as paradises for plants and animals, but they can be dangerous as well. Predators are always on the prowl, and hiding during the day is one way to stay alive.

VOCABULARY
A *predator* is a hunter.

Of course, many predators are also nocturnal. Bats are a perfect example. Over forty-two kinds live in and around the rain forest I was visiting. Some eat fruit or nectar from flowers. Others prey on insects. These bats use their sophisticated sonar and sense of hearing to snatch nocturnal insects off leaves or right out of the sky.

Daddy-longlegs, frogs, and scorpions are also nighttime hunters. My favorite nocturnal predators, though, live in underground burrows about as wide as a half dollar. Walking quietly, my group and I sneaked up on one of these burrows. Sitting at the entrance was a red-legged tarantula—a princely predator if I ever saw one.

The tarantula was about the size of my palm, and it lay in wait for a tasty cockroach or other creature to come by. When it did, the tarantula would pounce, injecting its venom into the prey and dragging it into its burrow for a feast. The tarantula was no threat to us—just the opposite. When we came too close, it scurried into its den until the dangerous pack of "two-legged giants" had moved on.

VOCABULARY
Venom is a poison.

We saw so many creatures that before I knew it, my watch read eleven o'clock. Our guide shone a flashlight on a branch, and we saw the rump of a sleeping bird called a bush tanager. I decided that the bird had the right idea. It had been fun to see so many nocturnal rain forest animals, but I realized I was not one of them. Yawning, I said good night to my guide, the rest of my group, and the rain forest creatures. Then I hiked back to my hotel and went straight to bed.

The Empty Pot

by Demi

A long time ago in China there was a boy named Ping who loved flowers. Anything he planted burst into bloom. Up came flowers, bushes, and even big fruit trees!

Everyone in the kingdom loved flowers too. They planted them everywhere, and the air smelled like perfume.

The Emperor loved birds and animals, but flowers most of all, and he tended his own garden every day.

But the Emperor was very old. He needed to choose a successor to the throne. Who would his successor be? And how would the Emperor choose? Because the Emperor loved flowers so much, he decided to let the flowers choose.

The next day a proclamation was issued: All the children in the land were to come to the palace. There they would be given special flower seeds by the Emperor. "Whoever can show me their best in a year's time," he said, "will succeed me to the throne."

This news created great excitement throughout the land! Children from all over the country swarmed to the palace to get their flower seeds.

All the parents wanted their children to be chosen Emperor, and all the children hoped they would be chosen too!

When Ping received his seed from the Emperor, he was the happiest child of all. He was sure he could grow the most beautiful flower.

Ping filled a flowerpot with rich soil. He planted the seed in it very carefully. He watered it every day. He couldn't wait to see it sprout, grow, and blossom into a beautiful flower!

Day after day passed, but nothing grew in his pot.

Ping was very worried. He put new soil into a bigger pot. Then he transferred the seed into the rich black soil.

Another two months he waited. Still nothing happened.

By and by the whole year passed.

Spring came, and all the children put on their best clothes to greet the Emperor. They rushed to the palace with their beautiful flowers, eagerly hoping to be chosen.

VOCABULARY

To *sprout* is to grow up quickly.

VOCABULARY

If something was *transferred*, it was moved from one location to another.

Ping was ashamed of his empty pot. He thought the other children would laugh at him because for once he couldn't get a flower to grow.

His clever friend ran by, holding a great big plant. "Ping!" he said. "You're not really going to the Emperor with an empty pot, are you? Couldn't you grow a great big flower like mine?"

"I've grown lots of flowers better than yours," Ping said. "It's just this seed that won't grow."

Ping's father overhead this and said, "You did your best, and your best is good enough to present to the Emperor."

Holding the empty pot in his hands, Ping went straight away to the palace.

The Emperor was looking at the flowers slowly, one by one.

How beautiful all the flowers were!

But the Emperor was frowning and did not say a word.

Finally he came to Ping. Ping hung his head in shame, expecting to be punished.

The Emperor asked him, "Why did you bring an empty pot?"

Ping started to cry and replied, "I planted the seed you gave me and I watered it every day, but it didn't sprout. I put it in a better pot with better soil, but still it didn't sprout! I tended it all year long, but nothing grew. So today I had to bring an empty pot without a flower. It was the best I could do."

When the Emperor heard these words, a smile slowly spread over his face, and he put his arm around Ping. Then he exclaimed to one and all, "I have found him! I have found the one person worthy of being Emperor!

"Where you got your seeds from, I do not know. For the seeds I gave you had all been cooked. So it was impossible for any of them to grow.

"I admire Ping's great courage to appear before me with the empty truth, and now I reward him with my entire kingdom and make him Emperor of all the land!"

All About...
BOOKS

If a Roman emperor wanted to read a book, he had to unroll it. Books were written on long scrolls (kind of like a roll of paper towels) that you unrolled as you went along. This was clumsy, especially if you were looking for a certain passage. Around A.D. 100 the codex was invented. It was made up of a stack of pages stitched together at the side and protected by a cover. The codex was easier to carry around, to store, and to search through. Books we read today look something like a codex.

In the Middle Ages, books were made by monks who copied them by hand onto prepared animal skins called parchment. The monks often decorated the pages with beautiful color illustrations called "illuminations." Books were scarce, and few people who were not priests or monks could read. Even those who could read had to be rich to buy these handwritten books.

A big change came with the use of paper and printing, which were first invented in China. Paper came into Europe through the Muslim world and was common by the 14th century. Johann Gutenberg of Germany perfected printing in the 1450s. Once books no longer had to be copied by hand and could be printed on paper, they became less expensive and reading became more common.

At first books were still not easy to make and not cheap. Each letter was on a separate piece of type, and a typesetter had to put each piece into place individually. Once all the letters for the page were in place, they were covered with ink and printed, one at a time, by hand on a press. By the 19th century, however, steam-powered presses could print out hundreds of pages at a time. Another invention was the linotype machine, which stamped out individual letters and set them up much faster than a typesetter could. Now books had become truly affordable, and the skill of reading was something that everyone was expected to learn.

Farming in SPACE

Can we grow food on a space voyage?

by Amy Hansen

What will astronauts eat when a space voyage takes years or even decades?

Lots of fresh vegetables, says Dr. Mary Musgrave of the University of Massachusetts. She has spent the last 10 years learning how to grow plants in space. And it's a good thing she has already started her work, because extraterrestrial gardening can be tricky.

In 1997, while the Mir Space Station spun around Earth, astronaut Mike Foale peered at a sealed growth chamber. The astronaut had planted Dr. Musgrave's quick-growing seedlings in the chamber, but none of the stems were showing.

Confused Plants

He opened the container and saw the problem. The white stems weren't growing upward. Instead, they threaded downward or sideways. Some of the roots snaked up, while others twisted around. These were confused plants.

On Earth, a plant's roots and stems take cues from gravity, using the Earth's pull to find "up" and "down." This process is called *gravitropism*. On the Mir, there was almost no gravity.

Dr. Musgrave suggested a solution: give the plants more light. This idea made sense because plants also use sunlight to find their way—a process called *phototropism*.

And it worked. Once the seedlings had more light, the stems turned up and the roots went down.

Now Dr. Musgrave was free to worry about the next problem: Would her baby plants live to flower?

Starving for Air

Many plants died in space. But Dr. Musgrave thought she knew why. She thought the space plants were starving for air.

Plants live by taking up carbon dioxide from the air. Since a plant uses up this gas in the air around it, the plant needs air currents to bring more carbon dioxide close to its surface.

On Earth, the air is always moving. Gravity pulls down cold air, and warm, lightweight air rises. So the air is shifting even when we can't feel a breeze. And with these shifts, plants get plenty of carbon dioxide.

Air Currents

Many earlier experiments with plants in space had used closed chambers. On the Mir Space Station, Dr. Musgrave tried a new greenhouse that had a fan pulling in a constant supply of the air inside the space station.

The plants loved it. They flowered and even produced more seeds, which Mike Foale was able to plant and grow. Using Dr. Musgrave's method, he completed the first seed-to-seed experiment in space, and moved one plant closer to an extraterrestrial garden.

"And this," says Dr. Musgrave, "is good news for long-term space travel."

The Little Red Ant
AND THE GReat
BIG CRUMB

A Mexican Fable

retold by Shirley Climo

Once, in a cornfield in Mexico, there lived a little red ant. She shared an anthill with her nine hundred ninety-nine cousins. They looked exactly alike except for the little red ant. She was a bit smaller than the others.

Early one fall morning all the ants crawled from their anthill. They paraded single file across the field, looking for food to store for the winter. Because her legs were shorter, the little red ant was last in line.

"¡Amigos!" she called. "Wait for me."

"Quick!" scolded the others. "¡Pronto!"

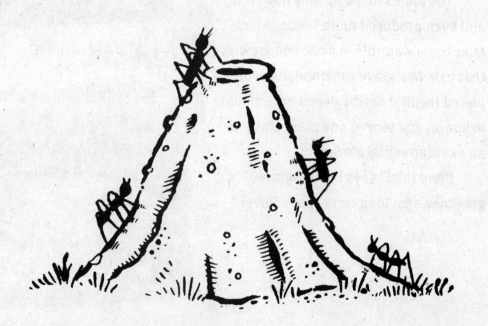

"Stay a while," La Araña coaxed, "and keep me company."

The little red ant gazed up at the spider. The sun had moved higher in the sky and no longer seemed caught in the web. A fly was caught instead.

"No, gracias," said the ant quickly. She did not want La Araña to tie her up like the fly. "No, thank you."

The little red ant backed down the stalk and hurried on her way. She had not gone very far when she stumbled over the roots of two tall thin trees.

"¿Qué pasa?" a scratchy voice demanded. "What's happening?"

The ant rubbed her eyes. She saw that the roots were really claws. She saw that the trees were really legs. She looked up and saw a fierce face with beady eyes bending over her. A yellow beak snapped open and shut, and a red topknot bobbed up and down.

The ant guessed at once what it was.

"¡El Gallo!" exclaimed the little red ant.

"Por favor . . ." the ant begged the rooster. "Please . . . don't eat me!"

"Ants taste HORRIBLE!" squawked El Gallo.

"Then will you carry my crumb of cake for me?"

"I'm too busy." The rooster cocked his head. "Did you say cake?"

"Sí," said the little red ant. "Yes."

"Cake tastes DELICIOUS!" crowed El Gallo. "I shall eat your crumb myself!"

"But . . ." the ant began.

"Where is it?" The rooster ran about in circles. "Awk!" he screeched suddenly. "Listen!"

"To what?" asked the ant.

"To that dreadful noise! It's the chicken-chaser! Awk!" Flapping his wings, the rooster flew up and over the cornstalks.

The ant was glad to see El Gallo go before he found her great big crumb. "Lucky me," said the little red ant, and hurried on her way.

She had not gone very far when she came upon something big and bristly. Its nose was pointed to the sky, and the dreadful noise was coming from its mouth.

The ant guessed at once what it was.

"¡El Coyote!" exclaimed the little red ant.

"¡Hola!" the ant shouted to the coyote. "Hello!"

El Coyote stopped in the middle of a howl and stared down his nose at the ant. "Don't bother me. I'm singing the sun a bedtime song." The coyote threw back his head, ready to howl again.

"You must be strong to sing so loudly," said the ant. "Will you carry my big crumb of cake for me?"

"Not now," said El Coyote. "Maybe tomorrow. Or next week."

"But that might be too late!"

Suddenly the coyote pricked up his ears, and the hair on his back stood on end. "¡Mira!" he yelped. "Look! It is the terrible Hombre!" El Coyote tucked his tail between his legs and dashed off through the cornstalks.

The little red ant was sad to see him go. Then she shrugged and started on her way again. But . . .

Something was moving down the row toward her. It wore boots on its feet and a straw hat on its head.

The ant guessed at once what it was.

"¡El Hombre!" exclaimed the little red ant.

From far away, the man looked too small to help even an ant. But the nearer he came, the larger he got. Soon he was taller than the cornstalks, and his shadow stretched halfway down the row. He grew so tall that the little red ant could not even see the top of his hat.

"¡Señor!" called the ant. "Please carry my cake for me."

The man did not hear her. He kept walking.

Now the little red ant looked up and saw something terrifying. The heel of his huge boot hung over her head.

"¡Alto!" exclaimed the little red ant. "Stop!"

The man did not hear her. He kept walking. So . . .

The little red ant took a skip and a hop and caught hold of his shoelace. Then she ran up his leg.

The man rubbed his knee. So . . .

The little red ant scurried under his shirt.

The man scratched his chest. So . . .

The little red ant skittered over his shoulders.

The man slapped his neck. So . . .

The little red ant crept into his ear.

She shouted in her very loudest voice, "HELP ME!"

"Yi!" yelled the man. "Ticklebugs!" He shook his head and jumped up and down.

The straw hat flew from his head, and the little red ant tumbled down on top of it.

The man ran across the cornfield, still shouting, "TICKLEBUGS!"

The ant watched him go. "Adiós, señor," she called. "Goodbye." Then she thought of something quite surprising.

"I frighten El Hombre . . . who scares El Coyote . . . who chases El Gallo . . . who wakes El Sol . . . who warms El Lagarto . . . who can blow down an anthill. So . . .

"I AM THE STRONGEST OF ALL!"

The little red ant crawled off the hat. She followed her trail back through the cornstalks, just the way she had come. At last she reached her crumb of cake and pulled off the leaf.

"Aah," said the ant, sniffing. The cake was warm and sticky and smelled sweeter than ever.

She took a big, big breath. Then, ever so slowly, she lifted the crumb. She lifted it up and up until she could put it on top of her head. Then . . . Step by step,

inch by inch,

all by herself,

by the light of the moon,

the ant carried her wonderful cake home to the anthill.

She feasted on the crumb all winter long. And, when spring-time came . . . she was exactly the same size as her cousins.

"Lucky me!" exclaimed La Hormiga, the ant.

Anansi Goes Fishing

retold by Eric A. Kimmel

One fine afternoon Anansi the Spider was walking by the river when he saw his friend Turtle coming toward him carrying a large fish. Anansi loved to eat fish, though he was much too lazy to catch them himself. "Where did you get that fish?" he asked Turtle.

"I caught it today when I went fishing," Turtle replied.

"I want to learn to catch fish too," Anansi said. "Will you teach me?"

"Certainly!" said Turtle. "Meet me by the river tomorrow. We will go fishing together. Two can do twice the work of one."

But Anansi did not intend to do any work at all. "Turtle is slow and stupid," he said to himself. "I will trick him into doing all the work. Then I will take the fish for myself." But Turtle was not as stupid as Anansi thought.

Early the next morning, Turtle arrived. "Are you ready to get started, Anansi?" he asked.

"Yes!" Anansi said. "I have been waiting a long time. I want to learn to catch fish as well as you do."

"First we make a net," said Turtle. "Netmaking is hard work. When I do it myself, I work and get tired. But since there are two of us, we can share the task. One of us can work while the other gets tired."

"I don't want to get tired," Anansi said. "I'll make the net. You can get tired."

"All right," said Turtle. He showed Anansi how to weave a net. Then he lay down on the riverbank.

"This is hard work," Anansi said.

"I know," said Turtle, yawning. "I'm getting very tired."

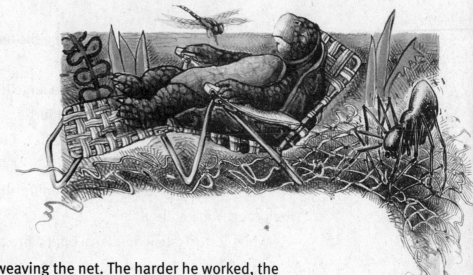

Anansi worked all day weaving the net. The harder he worked, the more tired Turtle grew. Turtle yawned and stretched, and finally he went to sleep. After many hours the net was done.

"Wake up, Turtle," Anansi said. "The net is finished."

Turtle rubbed his eyes. "This net is strong and light. You are a fine netmaker, Anansi. I know you worked hard because I am very tired. I am so tired, I have to go home and sleep. Meet me here tomorrow. We will catch fish then."

The next morning Turtle met Anansi by the river again. "Today we are going to set the net in the river," Turtle said. "That is hard work. Yesterday you worked while I got tired, so today I'll work while you get tired."

"No, no!" said Anansi. "I would rather work than get tired."

"All right," said Turtle. So while Anansi worked hard all day setting the net in the river, Turtle lay on the riverbank, getting so tired he finally fell asleep.

"Wake up, Turtle," Anansi said, hours later. "The net is set. I'm ready to start catching fish."

Turtle yawned. "I'm too tired to do any more today, Anansi. Meet me here tomorrow morning. We'll catch fish then."

Turtle met Anansi on the riverbank the next morning.

"I can hardly wait to catch fish," Anansi said.

"That's good," Turtle replied. "Catching fish is hard work. You worked hard these past two days, Anansi. I think I should work today and let you get tired."

"Oh no!" said Anansi. "I want to catch fish. I don't want to get tired."

"All right," said Turtle. "Whatever you wish."

Anansi worked hard all day pulling the net out of the river while Turtle lay back, getting very, very tired.

How pleased Anansi was to find a large fish caught in the net!

"What do we do now?" he asked Turtle.

Turtle yawned. "Now we cook the fish. Cooking is hard work. I think I should cook while you get tired."

"No!" cried Anansi. He did not want to share any bit of the fish. "I will cook. You get tired."

While Turtle watched, Anansi built a fire and cooked the fish from head to tail.

"That fish smells delicious," Turtle said. "You are a good cook, Anansi. And you worked hard. I know, because I am very, very tired. Now it is time to eat the fish. When I eat by myself, I eat and get full. Since there are two of us, we should share the task. One of us should eat while the other gets full. Which do you want to do?"

"I want to get full!" Anansi said, thinking only of his stomach.

"Then I will eat." Turtle began to eat while Anansi lay back and waited for his stomach to get full.

"Are you full yet?" Turtle asked Anansi.

"Not yet. Keep eating."

Turtle ate some more. "Are you full yet?"

"No. Keep eating."

Turtle ate some more. "Are you full yet?"

"Not at all," Anansi said. "I'm as empty as when you started."

"That's too bad," Turtle told him. "Because I'm full, and all the fish is gone."

"What?" Anansi cried. It was true. Turtle had eaten the whole fish. "You cheated me!" Anansi yelled when he realized what had happened.

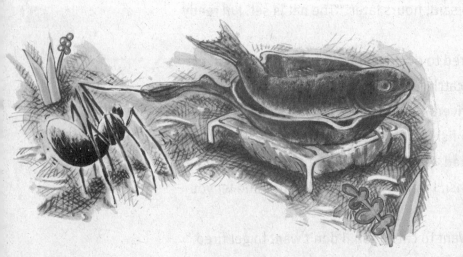

"I did not!" Turtle replied.

"You did! You made me do all the work, then you ate the fish yourself. You won't get away with this. I am going to the Justice Tree."

Anansi ran to the Justice Tree. Warthog sat beneath its branches. Warthog was a fair and honest judge. All the animals brought their quarrels to him.

"What do you want, Anansi?" Warthog asked.

"I want justice," Anansi said. "Turtle cheated me. We went fishing together. He tricked me into doing all the work, then he ate the fish himself. Turtle deserves to be punished."

Warthog knew how lazy Anansi was. He couldn't imagine him working hard at anything. "Did you really do all the work?" he asked.

"Yes," Anansi replied.

"What did you do?"

"I wove the net. I set it in the river. I caught the fish, and I cooked it."

"That is a lot of work. You must have gotten very tired."

"No," said Anansi. "I didn't get tired at all. Turtle got tired, not me."

Warthog frowned. "Turtle got tired? What did he do?"

"Nothing!"

"If he did nothing, why did he get tired? Anansi, I don't believe you. No one gets tired by doing nothing. If Turtle got tired, then he must have done all the work. You are not telling the truth. Go home now and stop making trouble."

Warthog had spoken. There was nothing more to be said. Anansi went home in disgrace, and it was a long time before he spoke to Turtle again.

But some good came out of it. Anansi learned how to weave nets and how to use them to catch food. He taught his friends how to do it, and they taught their friends. Soon spiders all over the world were weaving. To this day, wherever you find spiders, you will find their nets.

They are called "spider webs."

GENRE:
Biography

The Many Lives of
BENJAMIN FRANKLIN

written and illustrated by Aliki

Benjamin Franklin was born with just one life. But as he grew, his curiosity, his sense of humor, and his brilliant mind turned him into a man with many lives.

Benjamin Franklin was born in Boston in 1706. His mother and his father, who was a candlemaker, had many children. But they saw Ben was special. He was curious. He loved books. And even as a child, he was full of bright ideas.

Ben was always thinking—even at play. He liked to swim, and tried different ways. Once he made paddles so he could go faster.

Another time, when he was flying his kite near a pond, he had another idea. He went for a swim holding on to the kite string. Just as he thought, the kite pulled him across the water.

Ben loved school, but his parents did not have the money for him to continue. After only two years, he had to leave and choose a trade. It was decided that Ben would learn to be a printer like his brother, James. So when he was twelve, Ben was sent to live with him.

Ben learned quickly. He worked long, hard hours. Still, he found time to read every book he could borrow, and saved the money he earned to buy more.

At the shop, Ben wanted to do more than just help print his brother's newspaper. He wanted to write in it, too. So he thought of a way.

James began finding mysterious letters under the office door. They were signed "Silence Dogood." Silence wrote such funny stories, clever essays and poetry, James printed them. In fact, they helped him sell more newspapers. Little did he know that Silence Dogood was his little brother Ben.

But when James found out, he was angry. Ben was not allowed to write any more. He decided to go somewhere else, where he could write. So when he was 17, he left James and Boston.

Ben went to Philadelphia to start a life of his own. He found a job with a printer. He read and collected more books. He worked and saved until at last he bought his own shop. Now he could print his own newspaper and all the letters he wished.

A few years later, Ben met and married a young girl named Deborah Read. Deborah worked hard, too. She managed their new house, and her own general store next to Ben's print shop. Before long they had two children to help them.

Ben's newspaper was a great success. Then he began printing a yearly calendar called *Poor Richard's Almanack*. The booklet was full of advice, news, and information. What made it even more special were the wise, witty sayings of Poor Richard. Year after year, people bought the almanac. It made Ben famous.

Meanwhile, Benjamin Franklin was busy living other lives. He loved Philadelphia. It was a new city full of promise, and Benjamin was there at the right time. He started a club called the Junto, where friends met to discuss books and ideas.

He lent out his books, and soon others did the same. This began the first free lending library in America. He found new ways to light the streets, and to have them cleaned and paved, too. He started a police force, a fire department, a hospital, and an Academy. He helped make laws. Philadelphia became as famous as Benjamin Franklin.

By the time he was forty-two, Benjamin Franklin had enough money from his printing to live in comfort with his family. He gave up the shop to spend all his time with his ideas. A new life began.

Ben started scientific experiments, and soon became a master. He was the first to prove lightning was electricity. One day, during a thunderstorm, he tried a dangerous experiment with a kite and a key, and found he was right. He realized how to protect houses from lightning, and invented the lightning rod.

Benjamin Franklin made many discoveries in his lifetime, but he refused money for them. He said his ideas belonged to everyone. He wrote them down and they were translated into many languages. He became the best known man in America.

More than anything, Benjamin hoped people would listen to his most important idea—freedom for his country. For at that time, America was an English colony. He—and others—did not want to be ruled by England any longer.

He was sent to England to seek independence for his country. For eighteen long years, Benjamin stayed there and worked for that goal. In 1775, he returned to Philadelphia, sad and disappointed. His wife had died. War with England had begun, and America was still not free.

Yet he persisted. Benjamin Franklin and other great Americans helped Thomas Jefferson write the Declaration of Independence. They were determined to be free. But they knew they would first have to fight a long, terrible war. And they did.

But they needed help. Benjamin Franklin was old and weary when again he sailed away. This time he went to ask for aid from the King of France.

Benjamin was greeted as a hero. People in France knew about him and his inventions and they loved him. Finally, the King agreed. With his help, the war with England was won. America was free at last.

Benjamin Franklin had served abroad long enough. He wanted to spend his last years at home. When he finally returned from France, it was 1785. He thought he had been forgotten.

But he was not forgotten. He was greeted with wild celebrations. He saw his country still needed him. He became the first governor of Pennsylvania and helped write the Constitution of the United States.

Benjamin Franklin lived eighty-four years. He left the world his inventions, his ideas, his wisdom and his wit. He lived his many lives for us all.

VOCABULARY

If one *persisted*, he or she kept trying and did not give up.

VOCABULARY

To go *abroad* is to go to a foreign country.

by Patricia Daniels

The night sky is a glittering treasure house of glorious objects: stars, planets, galaxies, meteors, comets, and more. But to a beginning sky watcher, it can look like bright lights, dim lights, fuzzy lights, and moving lights. And that's on a good night. So, here's a quick guide to those lights in the sky. With this, a little practice, and a seasonal star chart in hand, you'll soon be able to tell a planet from a plane.

Stars are distinct, twinkly, unmoving points of light. On a dark, clear night in the country, you might see as many as 3,000 stars with the naked eye. In a city, only 200 or so are visible. Stars seem to twinkle because their light gets tossed around by our moving atmosphere. Star charts can help you identify them.

Planets, too, are considered unmoving points of light. Four of them can show up clearly at different times in the night sky: Venus, Mars, Jupiter, and Saturn. Brilliant white Venus appears in the early morning hours or in the evening, while Mars, the red planet, can show up at any time. Jupiter is not as bright as Venus, but this giant planet is brighter than any star, shining with a steady white glow. Saturn, not quite as bright as Jupiter, looks like a pale yellow star.

These planets don't twinkle the ways stars do. They are closer to Earth. Planets are always found along the ecliptic, which is the path

VOCABULARY
The *atmosphere* is the layer of gases that surround the earth.

across the sky followed by the Sun and Moon. Most star charts will show the ecliptic, although they won't show the planets, since their positions change from year to year.

Some lights in the sky are fuzzy. Take the Milky Way, for example. On a dark night, away from city lights, you'll see a blurry band of light across the sky. This is the main part of our galaxy, the Milky Way, and its light comes from a billion distant stars.

Galaxies, star clusters, and nebulas are some of the fuzzy lights that are scattered among the stars in blurry, glowing blobs. If you look at them closely with binoculars or a telescope, you'll realize that they are spectacular deep-space objects. Star clusters are dense collections of stars; the Pleiades, or Seven Sisters, are a good example. Nebulas are huge clouds of dust and gas where old stars blew apart or where new stars are born: the Orion Nebula is a stellar nursery. Galaxies are distant groups of billions of stars. The Andromeda Galaxy is the farthest object you can see with the naked eye, at 2.4 million light-years away.

Comets are the most easily recognizable "fuzzy light" objects. Every once in a while, an observer will spot what looks like a tiny piece of lint in the sky. If the fuzzy object changes position slightly from day to day, it could be a comet. "Comets appear fairly often and come without warning, but few are extremely bright or eye-catching," says Robert Burnham, author of *Great Comets*. "Comets aren't discovered until they come close enough to the Sun to 'turn on,'" Burnham says, "and that typically occurs only a few months at most before they're brightest." Astronomy Web sites are your best friends when it comes to identifying that bit of sky fuzz.

Meteors are moving points of light that you can see in the night sky. These fast-moving streaks, also known as shooting stars, are actually tiny chunks of space dirt that flame into vapor as they hit our atmosphere. Meteor showers occur at the same time each year as Earth swings through areas of comet dust in its orbit. Two of the best meteor showers are the Geminids, on November 16, and the Perseids, on August 12.

VOCABULARY
A *vapor* is a barely visible gas.

Airplanes are the most common moving points of light in the night sky, however. Aircraft move quickly across the sky, usually with flashing white or steady red and green lights. A few have steady white lights, but you'll be able to see that they are planes through binoculars.

Satellites, shuttles, and the space station can also be seen, if you look hard enough. Search for them just after sundown, when they are lit by the sunlight still high in the sky. They look like stars but move steadily across the sky, sometimes disappearing as they pass into Earth's shadow. Web sites can help you find out what's cruising over your area tonight.

However, if you should notice large, saucer-shaped hovering space vehicles in the night sky, the Galactic Imperium has asked me to assure you that these are just your imagination.

You Can Do Astronomy

Moon Watching

Believe it or not, some people think that there are several moons in the sky, probably due to its changing appearance during the month. Some cultures believe that the moon is born each month, slowly growing into adulthood (the full moon) and then dying (into a thin sliver), only to be reborn again.

Here's a little background on *why* the moon's phases occur. The moon travels around the earth, taking roughly one month to complete its journey. (Notice that the word "month" is similar to the word "moon.") At the same time, the earth is orbiting the sun. The two motions cause the sun, earth, and moon to be in different positions, relative to each other.

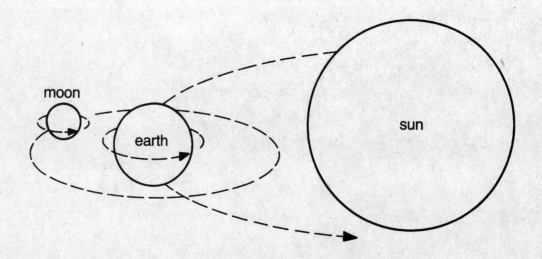

Like the earth and other planets of our solar system, the moon reflects the light of the sun. When the moon is aligned between the sun and earth, the illuminated side of the moon faces *away* from earth and the moon is not visible to observers on earth. We call this the "new moon" phase. As the moon moves out of alignment and continues its journey, we say that the moon is *waxing* (or getting bigger), and it becomes visible the next night as a thin sliver in the west, around sunset. This is called the *waxing crescent*.

One week after the new moon phase, the moon has completed one quarter of its journey around the earth. The moon appears half illuminated (but remember, we are only seeing half, so half of a half is a quarter); this is called the *first quarter* phase. You'll see the first quarter moon high in the south at sunset. (Notice that only the right side is illuminated.)

In the nights following the first quarter phase, look for the moon to appear more than half lighted, but less than fully so. This is the *waxing gibbous* phase. (The word "gibbous" means curved or "humped" moon.) You'll find the moon in the southeast at sunset.

VOCABULARY

If an object is *aligned*, it is forming a straight line with other objects.

VOCABULARY

If one side of the moon is *illuminated*, sunlight is shining on it.

Two weeks after the new moon phase, look for the *full moon* to rise in the east as the sun sets in the west. The bright full moon is visible all night and sets at sunrise. After the full moon phase, the moon appears to shrink. We say the moon is *waning*. Look for the *waning gibbous* moon to rise after sunset.

Three weeks after the new moon phase, the moon will be three quarters of its way around the earth. Observers on earth will see a half moon (this time, the left half of the moon is lighted). We call this the *third* or *last quarter* phase. The moon rises at midnight, and you might notice it during the daytime.

Next, the moon continues shrinking into the *waning crescent* phase. You may notice it rising a few hours before the sun. Finally, when the moon has completed its journey around the earth, it returns to the new moon phase.

The moon travels around the earth in a path that is tilted 5 degrees from the earth's path around the sun. This means that during the new and full moon phases, the earth, sun, and moon are nearly, but not exactly, aligned. Only when the alignment is exact do we see an eclipse.

Now that you know why it happens, it's time to learn to connect the moon's phase names with the moon's appearance. You'll need to find a calendar (but not one with the moon's phases already labeled!) or you could make your own. With an adult family member, go outside and find

VOCABULARY

An *eclipse* of the sun happens when the moon blocks the sun from view.

the moon. Now, using a moon phase chart, identify the moon phase that you see outside. Draw a picture of the moon's phase on the calendar. Try to make an observation each day, remembering that you may have to look for the moon at different times, depending on the phase. And don't worry if it's cloudy or rainy sometimes—just keep looking on the nights that are clear.

Use the moon phase descriptions (earlier in this section) and try to predict when the different phases will occur. Use a different-color pen or pencil to label your predictions and then, each day, check them with your own observations. Were you correct in your predictions? By watching the moon, you will become really good at identifying those moon phase names!

VOCABULARY

A *prediction* is something that is told before it happens.

SUNDAY	MONDAY	TUESDAY	WEDNESDAY	THURSDAY	FRIDAY	SATURDAY
			LAST QUARTER			
			FULL MOON			
			FIRST QUARTER			
				NEW MOON